D1058976

DISCARD

"What do courage, compassion and unbridled determination look like? The answer can be found in Lisa Lisson's *Resilience*. As the father of three girls, I often think of Lisa as a template for all that they might be able to achieve in life, even through very difficult times. *Resilience* is a must-read for anyone who wonders about the limits of the human spirit."

— JOHN DERRINGER, Q107 RADIO, TORONTO

"I loved reading Lisa's story — it is so inspirational! With great life lessons, from her incredible positive outlook to her relentless preparation, goal setting, organization and visualization of success, there is something in here for every leader, man or woman, who wants to learn to be more effective, to meet their goals and to conquer challenges, whether personal or professional."

— LINDA HASENFRATZ, CEO, LINAMAR CORPORATION

"I have known Lisa professionally for over a decade and always appreciated her direct and candid style. While I knew a little about her personal life, the full story as laid out in *Resilience* is a road map for the power of perseverance and overcoming seemingly insurmountable obstacles. It is also a powerful reminder of how to keep perspective, especially in those moments when our personal and professional lives collide."

— DENISE PICKETT, PRESIDENT OF U.S. CONSUMER SERVICES, AMERICAN EXPRESS COMPANY

Resilience

NAVIGATING LIFE, LOSS AND THE ROAD TO SUCCESS

LISA LISSON

Copyright © Lisa Lisson, 2017

Published by ECW Press
665 Gerrard Street East
Toronto, Ontario, Canada M4M 1Y2
416-694-3348 | info@ecwpress.com

All rights reserved. No part of this publication
may be reproduced, stored in a retrieval system,
or transmitted in any form by any process
— electronic, mechanical, photocopying,
recording, or otherwise — without the prior
written permission of the copyright owners
and ECW Press. The scanning, uploading, and
distribution of this book via the Internet or via
any other means without the permission of the
publisher is illegal and punishable by law. Please
purchase only authorized electronic editions,
and do not participate in or encourage electronic
piracy of copyrighted materials. Your support of
the author's rights is appreciated.

To the best of her abilities, the author has
related experiences, places, people, and
organizations from his memories of them. In
order to protect the privacy of others, he has, in
some instances, changed the names of certain
people and details of events and places.

LIBRARY AND ARCHIVES CANADA
CATALOGUING IN PUBLICATION

Lisson, Lisa, author
Resilience : navigating life, loss and
the road to success / Lisa Lisson.

ISSUED IN PRINT AND ELECTRONIC FORMATS.
ISBN 978-1-77041-398-6 (hardcover)
ALSO ISSUED AS: 978-1-77305-097-3 (PDF)
978-1-77305-098-0 (EPUB)

1. Lisson, Lisa. 2. Success in business.
3. Work-life balance. 4. Resilience
(Personality trait). 5. Loss (Psychology).
I. Title.

HF5386.L585 2017   650.1
C2017-902401-9 C2017-902980-0

Cover design: Tania Craan
Unless otherwise noted, all photos
are from the author's personal collection.

The publication of *Resilience* has been generously supported by the Government of Canada
through the Canada Book Fund. *Ce livre est financé en partie par le gouvernement du Canada.*
We also acknowledge the contribution of the Government of Ontario through the Ontario
Book Publishing Tax Credit and the Ontario Media Development Corporation.

Canada

PRINTED AND BOUND IN CANADA   PRINTING: FRIESENS   5   4   3   2   1

For Patrick.
My love,
my light,
my rock.
I miss you every single day.
Until our next Sunday morning . . .

To Hailey, Chloe, Mya and Jack.
You have helped me find happiness again.
I love you to the moon and back,
always and forever.

"Resilience is that ineffable quality that allows some people to be knocked down by life and come back stronger than ever."

— *Psychology Today*

CHAPTER ONE

Defining Moment

AROUND ONE O'CLOCK in the morning on Monday, August 13, 2007, I was awakened by the sound of a loud thump. When I looked to see what had caused it, I noticed my husband wasn't in bed. Puzzled, I turned on the bedside light. "Pat? Where are you?" No answer. I climbed out of bed and went around to his side. He was lying motionless on the floor as if someone had set him down there. "Pat, why are you on the floor?" No answer. I shook him. "Patrick, wake up." I shook him again. *Oh my god, what's wrong with him?*

I put my ear to his chest. Nothing. I felt for air under his nose. Nothing. My adrenaline was surging. I raced for

1

the phone, dialed 911, ran back to his side, put the phone on speaker and set it on the floor.

This can't be happening. Don't you die on me. Don't you dare die on me.

The dispatcher came on the line.

"I need help. My husband's lying on the floor. He's not breathing. Please help me do CPR."

"Help is on the way, ma'am. Is your front door unlocked?"

"Oh my god, no."

"You have to go and open it. Where are you in the home?"

"The master bedroom."

I run downstairs, disable the alarm, fling open the door, run back upstairs and kneel at Patrick's side.

"Okay I'm here. Tell me what to do."

The dispatcher tells me how to position myself, where to place my hands, how to lock my arms. His tone is calm, prescriptive.

"This is what you're going to do, ma'am. On the count of three, you're going to push down hard on your husband's chest. You're going to press down for three counts. Then you're going to release and start over. I'm going to count with you. Tell me when you're ready."

"I'm ready."

"Okay, here we go. One. Two. Three."

I press on Patrick's chest. One. Two. Three. Release. One. Two. Three. Release.

I repeat the cycle six, maybe seven times.

"Is he breathing yet?"

"No. Why isn't he breathing? Why isn't this working?"

"Keep going, ma'am. Stay with me."

One. Two. Three. Release. One. Two. Three. Release. "Come back, Patrick. Come back. Please. *Breathe*."

"Mommy, what's wrong with Daddy?" Chloe, our seven-year-old daughter, and Mya, her younger sister, are in the room. They can see their father on the floor. They can see me pressing on his chest. They can hear the dispatcher counting.

"Daddy's not feeling well, girls. The ambulance is coming. Can you guys go sit on the stairs and watch for the shiny lights?"

I say this in my mommy voice without breaking rhythm. They leave the room.

One. Two. Three. Release. One. Two. Three. Release.

"Is he breathing yet?"

"No. Why isn't this working?"

I hear footsteps on the stairs. Male voices. "God, there are kids here," one says.

A fireman is in the room. In one fell swoop he scoops me up by the waist, lifts me in the air and deposits me outside the bedroom where his partner is waiting with the kids.

"We've got this, ma'am. Take them downstairs." They go inside and shut the door behind them.

As we go down the stairs, the paramedics pass us going up. The foyer is swarming with uniforms. They're milling about, conferring in huddles, talking into walkie-talkies. The house looks like the command post for a military operation.

Two police officers are waiting for us at the bottom of

the stairs. A female officer leads us away from the commotion towards the kitchen and family room at the back of the house. We sit down on the couch. I have a clear view down the hallway to the foyer from where we're sitting.

"How many children are in the house?" she asks.

"Four. Two are still sleeping."

"How old are they?"

"Nine and three. Should I go and get them?"

"No, we're not going to wake them. Who can you call to be with you right now?"

I want to call my mom, but my parents just left for a Mediterranean cruise. Jojo, our nanny, lives down the street. I call her to come watch the kids.

The officer wants to know if Patrick suffers from any medical conditions or is taking any medications. No. Does he use any drugs? No again.

She asks how long we've been married.

"Thirteen years. It'll be fourteen in January."

"Is everything good between you both?"

At first I'm puzzled by her question. Then I understand. *She thinks maybe I did this. If Patrick's dead, maybe I killed him. Why else would my fit, thirty-eight-year-old husband be lying on the floor, not breathing?*

"Of course everything's good between us."

Jojo arrives. She takes the kids to another part of the family room. I ask her not to let them see me cry. As soon as they're gone, I head for the bottom of the stairs. I have to be there when they bring Patrick down. The officer bars my way.

Ten minutes pass. Fifteen.

"Why are they up there so long? Why aren't they rushing him to the hospital? Can you please go and ask them?"

"Let them do their work, ma'am. We're all here to support you. Relax. Take a breath."

Twenty minutes. Twenty-five. Thirty. I'm going out of my mind. I keep peering down the hallway trying to push my way past the officer, get to the stairway. *I don't understand. Why aren't they bringing him down?*

But they're not bringing him down.

The fear is coming in titanic waves now. I try to outrun it. *Please don't die. Please don't die. Please don't die.*

I glance at the wall clock. They've been upstairs for thirty-five minutes.

He's dead. I know it. They can't get a pulse. Why else haven't they brought him down yet?

I start sobbing.

Another voice vies for airtime in my head.

Lisa, pull it together. You don't know if they have a pulse. You don't have that information yet.

It's true. I don't know. I mustn't jump to conclusions.

I pull myself together.

"Please," I beg the officer. "Let me go. I need to be there when they bring him down."

Finally she relents.

I race down the hall and stand sentry by the staircase. More minutes pass. At last the bedroom door opens. A police officer comes down the stairs. He's young, early twenties maybe. When he reaches the bottom I cling to his arm like a lost child.

"All I need to know is if you have a pulse."

"Yes," he says. "We have a pulse."

IF YOU'D ASKED ME to describe my life before the sirens came screaming to our door, I'd have told you it was blessed. I was married to my best friend — my high school sweetheart and the love of my life. I loved my job as vice-president of marketing, customer experience and corporate communications at FedEx Express Canada, and Patrick loved his as director of marketing at CGC, a global building supply company. We had four kids — three girls and a boy, ages nine, seven, five and three — and a beautiful home in Burlington, Ontario, a community about forty miles west of Toronto. That weekend we'd just returned from our annual summer vacation in Muskoka.

We'd been renting cottages in Muskoka ever since Jack, our youngest, was an infant. That summer we'd rented on Lake Muskoka. We did all the cottagey things: swimming, boating, bonfires. We had music going all the time: The Police, Pearl Jam, U2. The kids knew the lyrics to all of our favourites. When we cranked up "Blinded By The Light" they loved to sing along with Manfred Mann.

The most striking thing about those two weeks was how spectacularly ordinary they were. I planned our meals and Pat shot the videos, just as we always did. He barbecued the steaks and I kept an eye on them so they wouldn't overcook, just as we always did. I handled cleanup and he readied the kids for bed, just as we always did.

The two weeks flew by. Saturday we drove home. Sunday we got organized for the week. Sunday night we had Pat's family for dinner. After they left, we tidied up. Then we sat on the patio for a while and shared a glass of wine. Work was always nuts after a vacation and with four small kids life sometimes felt like an endless Tilt-A-Whirl ride. We wanted to savour our last few moments together before heading back into the fray.

After we drank our wine we put the kids to bed. Around ten, we turned in ourselves. We were brushing our teeth when Pat became reflective.

"You know," he said, "you and I are so fortunate. We have such a great life. We have a wonderful marriage and family, careers we both love, interesting travel opportunities. We've already had more joy than most people manage to find in their entire lifetimes. Even at my age, I already feel as if I've lived a full life."

He went on in this vein for the next fifteen minutes. He was still talking about how blessed we were when we climbed into bed.

Pat was a sensitive guy, but I'd never heard him talk this way before. I wondered what had prompted him to become so philosophical all of a sudden.

"Pat, where is this coming from?" I asked.

"I don't know. I just wanted you to know how I feel."

"Well I feel the same way, baby. But it's after eleven. We have work tomorrow. Let's go to sleep."

I turned off the light and we slid beneath the covers.

THEY HAVE A PULSE. I'm standing at the bottom of the stairs, clutching the railing, waiting for the paramedics to bring him down, my emotions a jumble of fear and elation. I know the situation is dire. I know he's not out of the woods. But when I left him he wasn't breathing. *They have a pulse.*

Five minutes pass. Forty-five have elapsed since help arrived. The bedroom door opens. The paramedics bring him down. He looks tanned and handsome as they carry him past. I follow them out the front door into the buzzing commotion and flashing lights. Two fire trucks, two police cruisers, an ambulance and EMS vehicle are parked on the street in front of our house. The paramedics put him into the ambulance and shut the doors. They pull away, sirens blaring.

I'm still in my housecoat. I tell the officer I have to change before I leave for the hospital. She says she'll drive me. She has to stay with me until the doctors determine what happened. She motions for me to follow her upstairs and warns me not to touch anything in the room. Until the police hear from the doctors, the bedroom is considered a crime scene. I open the door. Bandages, plastic gloves, syringes and medical paraphernalia are strewn everywhere. The sight is deeply unnerving.

I throw on something to wear while the officer stands guard. Then I head downstairs to find Jojo, who's still waiting in the family room with Chloe and Mya. By some miracle, Hailey and Jack are still sleeping. I tell Jojo I need her to stay overnight, then leave her to deal with the children.

Joseph Brant, our local hospital, is a fifteen-minute drive from our house. When we arrive, the ambulance is parked in the emergency bay with its doors flung open. The paramedics are standing around outside. Pat is still inside.

"What's going on? Why aren't they rushing him in?"

"Don't worry," the officer says. "We're going in. We'll find out what's happening."

She leads me into a small private room to the right of the emergency waiting area and tells me to call someone to be with me. I call my brother Michael. People keep knocking on the door. Every time someone knocks, the officer gets up, leaves the room and shuts the door behind her. I wait. I worry. I watch the clock. I'm desperate for information. My mind keeps returning to the last conversation I had with Patrick before we went to bed. *Why was he so intent on telling me how grateful he was for his life? Did he know something was going to happen? Was he saying goodbye?*

I retrace his words searching for clues. I keep flashing back to the young police officer who told me that they had a pulse. His expression was completely devoid of encouragement. He didn't tell me not to worry. The paramedics had been upstairs for forty-five minutes by then. I wasn't stupid.

Almost two hours pass. Around four a.m. a nurse comes in and asks to speak to the police officer. They step outside the room and return a few minutes later. The nurse tells me Patrick had a heart attack. He is stable. I can see him. However, I shouldn't expect him to talk to me right now. The doctors have put him into a coma. The

9

officer tells me her job is done. She wishes me well, tells me to hang in there. Then she's gone.

The nurse takes me to Patrick. Nothing prepares me for what I see next. He is lying in the bed, his body a tangle of monitoring leads and IV lines. He is hooked up to so many machines it crosses my mind they had to hook him up to every one in the hospital just to keep him alive. My eyes go first to a huge metal monstrosity with a long plastic tube snaking out from it. The tube is taped to his face, inserted through his mouth and into his throat. The machine breathes rhythmically in and out and makes a wheezing sound. *Oh my god. He's not breathing on his own. This is not looking good.*

"What is all this?"

"A doctor will be in to talk to you."

I wait. A doctor comes in. He tells me Patrick had a heart attack. They have a heartbeat, but when his heart stopped beating it cut off the flow of oxygen to his brain and caused it to swell. They've put him into a coma to slow down his brain activity and reduce the swelling. At least that's what they hope will happen. They're doing the best they can.

I hear the doctor's words but I don't absorb their import. I'm still trying to process how seven hours earlier my husband and I were sitting on our patio sharing a glass of wine.

Later that morning the doctors move Pat from the ER to the ICU. All the other patients are at least thirty years older than him. I sit by his side and tell him he's going to pull through. I repeat this mantra again and again. I repeat it because I believe it is true. I don't think about what happens to a brain that's been starved of oxygen. I don't admit such thoughts into my consciousness. I allow only one thought: *Patrick is going to be fine. Patrick is going to wake up and be fine.*

I believe Patrick will wake up because Patrick is lucky. When he and his buddies go to Vegas, they lose; he wins. When Patrick goes to the track, he comes home with fist-fuls of cash. The guy has a horseshoe in his pocket. But he's not just a lucky gambler. Once his wallet fell out of his pocket on his way into a store and the next weekend he went back and found it lying in the snow. Things like that happened to Patrick all the time. He was one of those people who defied the odds.

For the next five days, I live at the hospital. Twenty-one hours a day I remain at Patrick's side. I leave only to go to the washroom. The other three hours I doze in the chair beside his bed or fall asleep fitfully on the waiting room couch.

Friends and family bring me fresh clothing, encourage me to eat. I'm not interested in eating. I'm interested in telling my husband he's going to be fine. When I have to cry, I leave the room. I have to cry a lot.

I keep telling myself I'm just having a bad dream. It must be a bad dream because something like this can't be happening to Patrick. To us. I instruct myself to wake up. But every time I wake up I realize it isn't a bad dream. Here I am. There's Patrick. This is real. It must be real. The pain is excruciating. I didn't know this kind of pain existed.

I'm afraid to go to sleep. If I go to sleep, I have to

wake up. If I wake up, I have to relive the horror. Either I have to awake from this nightmare or Patrick has to start talking. I don't care what happens first. I just want him to open his eyes and ask me what's for dinner.

I talk to the kids every day. They chatter away about their lives. I listen numbly. I tell them Daddy's sick and the doctors are trying to make him better. I say everything's going to be fine.

Tuesday, a friend of Patrick's comes to sit with him. He sobs the whole time. The next day he returns and sobs the whole time again. I ask him to leave. I tell him crying isn't going to serve any purpose right now. If Patrick hears him crying, he's going to think he's dying. He needs to believe that he's going to recover. And I can't have anyone around who brings me down.

Time slows. Machines bleep. The medical staff wanders in and out. Every day the nurses come in and test Patrick's brain activity. They take a pen and push it down hard on his nail cuticle. If he pulls his hand away, that's a good sign. It means he has reflexes. It means he's responding to pain. Every day they come in and push the pen down hard on his cuticle. Every day he just lies there. He doesn't flinch or move his hand away. The nurses never say "This isn't good." They don't have to.

Wednesday. I still haven't called my parents. I don't want to call them home from Europe until I know what I'm dealing with. By Wednesday, Patrick still hasn't responded to the pen test. I call. They make arrangements to fly home.

Patrick is receiving excellent care at Joseph Brant, but

I want him to receive the most specialized care available. I've learned that St. Michael's Hospital in Toronto has a brain trauma and neurosurgery unit staffed by a team of multi-disciplinary specialists. On Friday, the orderlies wheel him out to the helicopter pad and put him into an air ambulance to transfer him to St. Mike's. As it carries him away I tell myself everything's going to be fine. The doctors at St. Mike's will fix him.

After Patrick has been airlifted, I drive to my parents' place. They'd arrived home early that morning. As soon as I see my mom I fall apart in her arms. Then I pull myself together and tell her we have to hurry to the hospital. Patrick can't speak. I have to be his voice.

My mom and I had planned to sleep in the ICU waiting room but it's full when we arrive. We're going to need a plan B, but I can't deal with that right now. I'll have to figure something out later. Just then, a couple with whom Pat and I are close friends walks into the waiting room. The wife drops a set of keys into my hand. "There's a suite booked for you and your mom at Pantages Hotel," she says. "You're checked in and good to go." The hotel is a two-minute walk from the hospital. I'm so moved I cannot speak.

Hours go by. I can't read. I have no concentration. To pass the time I talk to the nurses and other families. The medics bring in a young man who's been in a terrible accident. He's even younger than Pat. I tell his family not to worry. He'll be okay. I tell everyone their loved ones will be fine. If I can convince them, I can convince myself.

On the weekend the doctors tell me they're going to

pull back on Patrick's drugs so they can bring him out of the coma. On Monday they'll try to wake him up to see if he has any brain activity. From that moment on I live in fear. The fear is far worse than any I've experienced during the past five days. It's so bad I can taste it. I can feel the doors closing. If the doctors at this hospital can't wake Patrick up, I have nowhere to turn.

I want him to wake up so badly. But he's not waking up. I'm desperate for him to open his eyes. But he's not opening his eyes. My mind keeps flashing back to that pen test. *Lisa, you need to be realistic. You need to think about that test.* Then it shifts gears. *Lisa, stay positive. You can't give up hope.*

Monday: Day Eight. I'm standing at Patrick's bedside, my mom at my side. The nurses wheel over a machine. The doctor says okay, let's see if we can wake him up.

They do one test after another. Patrick doesn't wake up.

The doctors tell me we need to have a meeting.

The room where we meet is sterile and windowless. It looks like the kind of room where you get bad news. Three doctors and a social worker are waiting when my mom and I arrive. The head neurologist lays out the facts. Patrick is in a vegetative state. He is severely brain-damaged. He will never wake up. What I'm seeing right now is what I will see for the rest of his life. If I keep him alive, he will have no quality of life. I need to consider whether he would want to live that way. They recommend that I let him go. They say they'll give us time to talk things over. They stand to leave.

I tell them I don't need time to think things over. I know my decision. It's so clear, so pure, so unvarnished, the force of my certainty is almost blinding.

"Do miracles happen in this hospital?" I ask.

"Yes," the neurologist says. "They happen every day."

"Then I need to know if I'm going to get mine."

IF I WERE TO PICTURE a map of my life, I'd visualize that moment as The Great Divide. I think of it that way because when the doctors gave me the news, a huge fault line opened up in my life. Everything leading up to that moment became my life before, everything that followed became my life after.

I didn't know it then, but the choice I made that day was the defining choice of my life. When I made it, when I decided there was no way that that beautiful man and my connection to him and all that we'd shared was going to end in that sad little room, I had no idea how the story would unfold. No map existed for what lay ahead. There weren't any guidebooks for me to follow. All I had was my steadfast love for my husband, my unerring faith that he'd defy the odds and my resolve to rewrite the ending of our story. But to tell you how that story began, I need to go back a bit.

CHAPTER TWO

Up, Down and Everything Between

I'M FOUR YEARS OLD. I'm sitting on the stairs in our house in Oakville, Ontario, watching my parents having a heated argument. Someone else is present, maybe a neighbour, although I'm not sure who it is or why that person's there. Voices are raised. I'm crying. "I can't live like this anymore," my mother says. "*I'm trying*. What do you want me to do?" my father replies. This is my first memory.

A year later I'm living in a house on the lakeshore in Burlington with my mom, my brother Michael, my mom's new boyfriend and his two sons.

MY PARENTS MARRIED WHEN they were both twenty-two. Dad got a job working in the mailroom at the Ford Motor Company. Mom took a job as an assistant for a local businessman. It was 1966. The following year my paternal grandfather bought a printing business in Brantford, a city about ninety kilometres southwest of Toronto. My grandfather didn't know anything about the printing business — he sold men's suit fabric to tailors for a living — but he bought the company, my grandparents moved to Brantford and my grandfather asked my dad to help him run the business. The business wasn't earning enough to pay Dad a salary at first, so my parents moved into the basement of my grandparents' home, my mom found an office job and my dad worked round the clock in the printing business.

Two years later, I was born. When I was a year old, my mom became pregnant with my brother Michael. My parents were still living with my grandparents, my dad still wasn't bringing home enough money for groceries, and my grandmother, who had rheumatic fever, kept asking my mom to keep me quiet during the day so she could nap. It wasn't exactly the life my mother had imagined for herself. By the fall of 1970 she'd had enough. With me in tow, and she seven months pregnant with Michael, my mother left my father, moved back in with her parents in Oakville and told them she was never going back.

My mom's father owned a metalworking company. One of his claims to fame was that his company had constructed the framework for the geodesic dome at Ontario

Place. Hoping to help save my parents' marriage, my grandfather gave my dad a job and my grandparents set my parents up in a house a few blocks away from theirs. The following month my dad moved back in with us and began training as a metal worker. For my mother, it was a second chance.

Upset about my father's defection, my paternal grandfather began pressuring him to come back. Feeling torn between his father and his wife, and trying to please them both, my dad returned to the printing company before the year was out and began commuting daily between Brantford and Oakville. Money was tight again. My mother had to take in boarders to make ends meet. If Michael or I got sick, she had to ask my grandparents for money to buy medicine. In the fall, she left us in the care of a neighbour and found a secretarial job at a dentist's office in Oakville. Two years later, she asked my father for a divorce.

The year I started kindergarten my life went into free-fall. My parents sold the house in Oakville, my dad moved back in with his parents, and my mom rented a house in Burlington. She became romantically involved with the dentist she was working for, we moved into a house they bought together in Burlington and his sons, who were seven and two, lived with us on alternate weekends. Soon afterwards my father rented a townhouse in Brantford, and Michael and I began spending alternate weekends there. Later that year we met Dad's new girlfriend and her three-year-old son.

Nothing made any sense. Suddenly my dad was gone and I was living in a new house. Then I was living in another house with a person I was supposed to call my dad only I didn't want to call him my dad because I already had a perfectly good dad and this new dad was a total stranger. Besides, if I had to have another sibling I wanted a sister, not another brother, but all these brothers kept showing up. The worst part was that I had no control. I had to accept my new reality. But I didn't want to accept it. I wanted my life to go back to the way the way it was. I was angry with my parents for divorcing. I was especially angry with my mother, whom I blamed for the divorce and for making me have a stepdad and for looking so happy when my dad looked so sad. Except for school, my only happy memory from that entire year was that now we had a pool.

I loved school. I loved it for many reasons, but mainly because the order of the classroom offered me respite from the chaos everywhere else in my life. When I was seven, my dad married his girlfriend and she and her son moved into my dad's townhouse. When I was eight, my mom and stepdad got married, and his ten-year-old son began living with us full-time. When I was nine, my mom and stepdad had a son and I started attending a new school. When I was ten, my dad and stepmom had a son. Between the ages of five and ten I went from being the oldest to being ousted from top position and from having one brother to having six: one biological (Michael), three step (Michael, Andrew and Gary), two half (Ronnie and Bradley).

During those years, besides school, I found safe haven in the company of my maternal great-grandmother,

Mabel. She lived nearby so I spent a lot of time with her as a child. I cherished our time together. Whenever I visited, she made tea and gave me the little figurines that came in the Red Rose tea boxes. I amassed a huge collection. Sometimes she took out a can of Pledge and we dusted together while she regaled me with stories about her childhood growing up in England.

My great-grandmother had known a great deal of hardship in her life. The youngest of twelve, she eloped with an Italian boy when she was in her teens and was shunned by her family. Her son died in a tragic accident as a young man, her daughter predeceased her later on, and she was widowed early. Nevertheless, she bore her pain with grace and never let the sadness and disappointments of her life destroy her.

Even as a child I sensed her mental toughness. She had an aura about her that suggested nobody was going to tell her what to do or how to do it. She also had a wonderful sense of style. I thought she was the picture of elegance in her tailored suits with the fur collars, scarves and brooches, hats and gloves. I loved my maternal grandmother, too, but she had a defeated air about her, so I didn't gravitate to her in the same way. I was always drawn to the light.

My great-grandmother viewed the events of her life as her destiny. Whatever your fate, she believed that you had to find a way to embrace life again, and she always counselled me to do the same. After my parents' divorce, when I felt so lost and displaced, she said, "Lisa, your mom and dad are happy now. They've found their true loves. Now you have to find your own happiness. You can do that by accepting what you can't change, thinking about what brings you joy and focusing on that." Then she challenged me to find something about my new life that made me happy.

I couldn't imagine finding one thing to like about my new life. But I admired my great-grandmother, so I tried to come up with something. At first, I kept thinking about everything I hated. But then I realized I actually did like a few things, like our new pool and my new canopy bed and getting to celebrate two birthdays and two Christmases. Out of a desire to please her I tried to focus on the positives.

Eventually I began to adjust to my new life. I came to accept my stepdad, Ron, who was a bright, hardworking man for whom nothing was more important than family, and who, from day one, treated me like one of his own children. I also began to accept my new brothers. We bickered from time to time as siblings do, but for the most part we got along. And other than that one argument I'd witnessed between my parents, I never heard them fight or disparage one another again.

After my dad moved into the townhouse, I counted the days until it was time to see him. The moment I spotted his brown-panelled station wagon parked outside the school on Friday afternoons, I raced to give him a hug. For the better part of the first year after my parents split, I felt sorry for my dad. I felt bad that he was the one who had to drive to see us all the time, that his house was so dark and sparsely furnished while ours was so spacious and airy, that his fridge was always bare except for a jug of milk and stack of TV dinners, while ours was always crammed with food. Then he met Joan. After that, his spirit blossomed and his fridge overflowed.

I don't have any memories of my parents as a happy couple. But from around age seven, I have many memories of both sets of parents and stepparents holding hands and kissing and of two stepparents who embraced Michael and me. Since both of my stepparents had parents who owned cottages, during the summers we headed to Ron's parents' place in Minden and Joan's parents' place in Normandale on Lake Erie. Mom and Ron bought a house in Florida. Sometimes we went there on vacations, while other times Dad and Joan took us camping in Killbear and Long Beach Park. And then there were those two birthday parties and Christmases I got to have every year. So as upset as I was at first about my parents' divorce, eventually I came to view it in a very positive light. The only part I hated — and I hated it with a passion — was travelling by train to Brantford on Christmas Day.

Shortly after my ninth birthday, my mom went into labour fifteen weeks prematurely and gave birth to my brother Ronnie. At birth, Ronnie weighed one pound, eleven ounces, had a collapsed lung and was blind in one eye. The doctors didn't know if he had brain damage. They gave him less than a ten percent chance of surviving.

I froze the first time I saw him. He was so tiny I could have fit him into the palm of my hand. His frail little body was a tangle of tubes and wires, and he had to breathe through a breathing machine. He was the most helpless looking creature I'd ever seen. We had to outfit ourselves in sterile gear from head to toe, put on special gloves and reach through the rubber hand in the incubator just to hold him.

A couple of weeks after Ronnie was born, my aunt also gave birth to a baby boy. She was allowed to bring her baby home from the hospital a few days later, while Ronnie lay in an incubator fighting for his life. *It isn't fair*, I kept saying. *Why does Aunt Joanna get to bring her baby home and ours has to stay?* I must have asked my mom and Ron that question a thousand times. But nobody ever gave me a satisfactory answer.

Ronnie hovered between life and death for four months. Finally the doctors let him go home. Today, except for his blindness in one eye and a few scars where his lung collapsed, he's healthy and normal. He's been followed and studied his entire life. *W5* did a story about him. "He's our miracle baby," my mom used to say. "I got my miracle."

IN GRADE FIVE, my mom and Ron decided to send me to St. Mildred's-Lightbourn School in Oakville. It was a strict girls' school. We had to wear uniforms and Oxford shoes. But I flourished in the structured environment and excelled at the academics and competitive sports.

I loved St. Mildred's, so when Mom and Ron decided to send me to Nelson High School in Burlington for grade nine, I put up a huge fight. None of my friends were going to Nelson. For once I didn't want my life to change. But they wanted me to experience a co-ed school and reasoned grade nine was the best time to make the switch since students would be filtering in from many schools that year. They asked me to try it for a year. If I didn't like it, I could return to St. Mildred's.

In the fall of 1982, I went to Nelson. I was miserable. I didn't know a soul. I didn't like co-ed classes. I was painfully self-conscious about my braces.

And then, on the second day, I met a boy.

I'd noticed him on the first day, actually. I'd caught him staring at me in some of my classes. His staring made me uneasy. *Who is this guy?* I wondered. *And why does he keep looking at me?* I only managed a stolen glance, but I saw he was cute. That much I registered.

I always arrived at class early, so I was sitting at my desk the following day when he entered the classroom. It was the second class of the morning. Geography class. He came in after the teacher had shut the door. I will never forget his entrance. He was wearing jeans, a concert tee, a black leather jacket and motorcycle boots. His hair was layered and longish, grazing his shoulders in that rocker way. He was so charismatic he took my breath away.

He scoped the room, spotted me, and sat down beside me. I could tell he was going to say something. Part of me desperately wanted him to and the other part was terrified that he might.

I had no experience with boys like him. The crowd I ran with viewed rockers as rebels. My brothers all went to private school. I was used to guys in suits.

Don't talk to me. Please don't talk to me.

"Hey," he said. "Can I ask you a question?"

I turned towards him nonchalantly.

24

"How do they get those silver things to stay on your teeth?"

Oh my god. He did not just ask me that.

I wanted to crawl under my desk.

I smiled nervously and looked away, but not before noticing he had the most piercing blue eyes I'd ever seen.

We had history next. He was in that class, too. He was in a lot of my classes. He kept showing up and sitting beside me. Eventually, we started talking. He told me his name was Patrick but his friends called him Pat. The more we talked, the more he intrigued me.

First there were those eyes. They were a striking aqua blue. Then there was his smile, which was irresistible. But it wasn't just his looks that I found captivating. His eyes radiated warmth. I'd seen that warmth there the first day he spoke to me and I'd sensed an openheartedness about him. A generosity of spirit. I could tell I wasn't just dealing with a good-looking jerk.

I started looking forward to seeing him and being disappointed when he didn't show up. When he did, the butterflies also showed up in full force. Within a month, I went from telling my mother, "I can't believe you're making me go to this school" to "I met a guy."

I pointed him out to her for the first time when she was driving me to school one morning. He was carrying his skateboard and walking down the street with his rocker buddies. She was so taken aback when she saw him she drove up on the curb and back down again. When I was older, and especially when I became a parent, I realized that she could have said many things to me that day, one of which might reasonably have been, "Over my dead body!" But she never said a word. Whatever her feelings, it wasn't her style to weigh in on such matters. She always allowed me to make my own decisions.

Towards the end of the fall, Patrick asked me if I wanted to go for a ride with him and his friend Steve to listen to some music. We'd never been together outside of school before. Steve was older and had a car so the three of us and another guy drove to a park near the school. Steve had a huge boombox. He put on Led Zeppelin and we hung around listening to music for a while.

Later, Steve drove me home and Pat walked me to the front door. When we got to the door, he leaned over and kissed me. I practically levitated with joy. It wasn't the first time I'd been kissed by a boy. But it was the first time a boy had inspired such crazy feelings.

The next day he came up to me at my locker, shoved a note in my hand and ran away. Inside, he'd scribbled *I just want to tell you you're so pretty and I really like you and I want to keep hanging out.*

And so it began.

We were the unlikeliest of couples. And at first we got labelled as the rocker dude and the preppy girl. People would say to him, "Oh, you're going for the preppy girl." But Patrick didn't care what others thought. If he was going after the preppy girl, then he was going after the preppy girl and too bad what anyone thought. I loved that about him. As it turned out, my first impressions of him couldn't have been more wrong. His tough guy persona totally belied the person he was. I loved that about him, too.

We went together through grades nine and ten. After grade ten we decided to take a break and date other people. That summer I ran into him and his buddies at a local fair. At first I didn't recognize him. He'd gone completely punk rock — mohawk, goth makeup, silver chains, Doc Martens, the whole bit. But even sporting a full-on punk look he was still good-looking, and as soon as we started talking the butterflies showed up en masse.

Later that summer I ran into him again at the mall. He told me he missed me and wanted to get back together. I said I missed him and wanted to get back together, too, but first I had one request: Would he mind toning down his new look a bit? I said I wasn't just asking for me. I was asking for my parents. I thought it might be a tough sell. I didn't see him again until the first day of school. When he came walking towards me in the hall, my mouth fell open. The mohawk was gone. He had on Levis, a baby blue Oxford cloth shirt and a pair of brown leather deck shoes.

In grade eleven we officially became an item. He made the football team and started attracting buzz. Girls began to take notice. If he'd been arrogant, he might have turned into a colossal jerk at that point. But his humility kept him grounded.

He had an irrepressible confidence and optimism. People naturally gravitated towards him. He was the life of the party. He didn't sit around telling jokes. He wasn't "on" all the time. He just had a way of telling a story that got people laughing.

For the next few years we did what high school kids do: hung out with friends, studied together, went to prom. He was smart, but not in an academic way: school wasn't his thing. I influenced him to apply himself more. I'm social and I like to have fun but I'm more on the serious side. He lightened me up a little.

I'm also a straight arrow. I can't break even the simplest rule, but Pat had a way of using his charm to get to the front of the line. "Come on," he'd say. "It's not going to kill you." But I always felt that cutting in was unfair to the people who'd been waiting longer. I break out in hives just thinking about it. He used to tease me a lot about stuff like that.

We rarely fought. If we did, it was usually because I wanted him to buckle down more. It drove me crazy when he didn't take his schoolwork seriously enough. As much as I loved his easygoing nature, at times it was a little too easygoing for my organized personality.

We were in love, but we never let our love define us as a couple. Sometimes when couples start going out they drop all their friends, and their friends start thinking, oh, for the love of god, can you please unglue yourself for five minutes and spend some time with us? We were not that couple. We had a few friends in common, but mostly our circles didn't intersect, so Friday nights we often went our own ways and met up later for a burger. It wasn't conscious. It just happened that way. We ebbed and flowed together through life.

Pat also came from a tight-knit family. He was the youngest of four. His dad was an electrician. His mom worked as a cashier in a local grocery store when I met her. She was Italian and a strong presence in his life. He'd never have dreamed of crossing her.

Once we started dating, my mom and Ron embraced him like another son. He practically moved in with us. Spending time with my family exposed him to a world he'd never encountered. When he came with us on vacation to Florida one year it was the first time he'd ever travelled on an airplane. He used to tell me all the time that it was the life he wanted for his own family. When it became clear that his family would also be mine, he said he was determined to create that life for us.

After high school, I decided to pursue a marketing degree at the University of Guelph. Pat didn't have the grades for university, so he lived at home and enrolled in a diploma course in marketing at Sheridan College in Oakville. He hoped for a career in sales and figured marketing was the best route.

University was basically four years of everything I loved: learning, socializing and making new friends. I threw myself into all three endeavours with enthusiasm. Weekends, either Pat drove up to campus or I went home. If I had to pull an all-nighter to cram for an exam, he partied with my friends. It was effortless, just like in high school. Minus the all-nighters, my first three years of university were bliss.

And then, in August, shortly before I was about to head back to school for my fourth year, Joan called. My dad was in the hospital. He'd blacked out just as he was about to get into his car after work. A few weeks later he had surgery. The doctors found brain cancer. They told him he had months to live.

I spent my final year of university struggling to keep my grades up, poring over medical journals to find a cure even though I knew none existed, and crying myself to sleep. Whenever possible, I accompanied Dad to London, Ontario, for his chemo treatments. Joan drove while I sat in the back seat holding his vomit bag. All he wanted was to make it to my graduation in early June. He died at forty-seven, on May 26, a few weeks short of his goal.

CHAPTER THREE

"This Is Not the Way
This Is Supposed to End"

WHEN THE DOCTORS AT ST. MIKE'S told me Pat was in a vegetative state and I chose to keep him alive, I know they didn't like my decision. They had given me statistics and probabilities of his recovery, with percentages so low they might as well have told me it was impossible. When I started talking about a miracle, I could tell they thought I was delusional. They asked if I was sure of my decision and whether it was the one Pat would want me to make. They said I had to think about whether he would choose to live that way. I needed to understand the long hard road I had ahead of me.

But when the doctors gave me Pat's prognosis, I didn't

visualize him spending the rest of his life on a ventilator. I pictured him opening his eyes and making a full recovery. After he recovered, I pictured him going on the speaking circuit and inspiring others with his story, like Tony Robbins. Maybe other patients with brains as damaged as his would never recover, but he was the miracle man, the guy with the horseshoe in his pocket. Pat would defy the odds. That's what I told him. That's what I told myself. And that's what I told everyone else.

AS RESOLUTELY OPTIMISTIC AS I WAS that Pat would pull through, I wasn't blind to the direness of his situation, especially after he'd failed to respond to the pen test. So while I'd hoped for the best during those first eight days, I also looked at his living will.

Pat and I had had wills drawn up after we'd started having kids. At the time, we'd both signed advance care directives indicating our wishes should either of us ever become too incapacitated to make care decisions for ourselves, and appointed each other as our substitute decision-makers. Pat's directive stated that he didn't want any extraordinary measures taken to prolong his life if no chance existed for him to live it in a meaningful way.

His wishes, then, were clear. And yet, when you sign a directive, you not only entrust your decision-maker with the responsibility of honouring your wishes when the time comes, you also charge them with the responsibility of interpreting your wishes within the context of the cir-cumstances in which a decision must be made. And there

I found myself wading into murkier waters. I wondered if when Pat had signed his directive he'd contemplated a life-and-death decision having to be made when he was in the prime of his life. If he'd anticipated that scenario unfolding only when he'd reached old age, might he have reconsidered his instructions? That question weighed heavily on me. My mind also kept circling back to the profound talk he'd had with me the night before his heart attack. I kept wondering if he'd had a premonition about his fate that night. Did he know what was coming? Was he trying to send me a message? If so, what was it? And how was I to interpret it?

My head swirled. What if I let Pat go and, when the kids were older, they asked me why I'd given up on their dad so soon? I couldn't answer that question. All I knew was that the doctors didn't know everything. Nobody believed my brother Ronnie would survive and his case had been written up in medical journals. If Mom had succeeded in getting her miracle, why couldn't I get mine? Besides, researchers were learning more about the brain every day. A new treatment could be just around the corner. With a brain trauma anything could happen. And sometimes you heard about those outliers who were comatose for years before they awakened. If anyone had the potential to be an outlier, it was Pat. I simply refused to believe that his luck had run out.

I thought about how Pat had always trusted me to make the big decisions in our lives. How if we'd differed on anything major, he'd always deferred to my judgment. Now I was charged with making the most critical decision

I'd ever had to make. When I decided to keep him on life-support, I remember thinking, "Sorry, Pat, I'm over-ruling you on this one."

The doctors weren't the only ones who thought I was delusional. Some people advised me to let Pat go, even though I didn't ask for their advice. Others said nothing, but their silence spoke volumes. I could see the skepticism in their eyes. Most people, though, had no idea how to react. It wasn't just how shocked they were that Pat had had a heart attack so young; it was that the heart attack hadn't killed him. My husband was gone but he wasn't gone. They didn't know what to say, so they just averted their eyes.

I didn't judge them. Under the circumstances, I'm not sure that I would have known how to respond either. I had less patience, though, for the people who didn't think before they spoke, such as those who wondered how Pat was getting along and when I expected him to come home from the hospital. Or the ones who inquired, "How are you doing?" I have no doubt they meant well, but my husband was in a vegetative state. I wasn't sure how I was supposed to answer that question.

The worst, though, were the people who offered me bromides. I heard, "This too shall pass" and "Time heals all wounds" so many times I told my mother that if one more person spoke those words to me I'd scream. I know the people who offered them did so with the best of intentions. I know they believed their words would give me solace. But all they did was profoundly upset me. I was walking around with a gigantic knife stuck through my heart. Even if time did heal all wounds, the idea that anything could ever heal the gaping hole in my heart was inconceivable to me. With my wound so fresh, those words were the last I wanted to hear. What I did appreciate hearing was that they couldn't imagine what I was going through or were only a phone call away if I needed anything. Beyond that, there really wasn't anything anyone could say. I was inconsolable.

The only person I could imagine having anything useful to say to me was someone who'd lived through the nightmare I was living, and I was desperate to find that person. I was alone in my anguish. Even my mother, who'd always been my north star, was powerless to help me there. My mother, who'd never once questioned my decision to keep Pat alive or told me to sleep on it or tried to talk me out of it, even when the doctors took her aside and told her that her daughter was in for a long haul. Still, my mother's words were the only ones that gave me any solace. "Baby," she said, "it isn't about what happens to you in life. It's about what you choose to do in response to what happens. Remember. You still have choices. You still have control to some degree."

WHATEVER THE DOCTORS AT ST. MIKE'S may have thought about my decision, they respected my right to make it and allowed me to do what I had to do. Since there was nothing more they could do for Pat, they sent him back to Joseph Brant. The doctors there performed a tracheotomy and inserted his feeding tube.

In the weeks and months that followed I was still largely in shock and functioning on autopilot. I no longer felt as if I inhabited my own life — I felt as if I were watching a movie of someone else's. I resumed my routine of travelling between home and hospital. The only difference was that I didn't stay overnight.

For the first few nights after Pat's heart attack, my neighbours took the kids; then my brother and his wife moved in until my mom returned from Europe. Jojo was already chauffeuring them to and from school, arranging their play dates and keeping the household going. She carried on with her duties during the week and picked up some of the chores that Pat and I would normally have handled on the weekends. Evenings, my parents took over. Either they put kids to bed at the house and waited until I came home, or they took them to their place and I drove straight there from the hospital and slept over. With Pat on the road so much for work, my parents usually took the kids a couple of nights a week anyway, so apart from spending more nights with my parents, for my kids it was business as usual.

Since I was already managing alone weekdays due to Pat's travel schedule, I found it easier to cope with his absence during those times. Weekends were unbearable. Pat had always been home on the weekends and we'd cherished that time together. Once we'd knocked off our chores, he'd tinker in the garage or rake the leaves while I puttered around the house. After his heart attack the hard part wasn't managing the chores. The hard part was waking up on weekend mornings and realizing he wasn't there to make breakfast for the kids or put smiley faces on their pancakes. Weekends, it was his presence I missed the most.

I took the kids to see Pat for the first time after he was back at Joseph Brant. The kids knew that their dad was sick and that the doctors were trying to make him better, but they were too young to understand the severity of his situation. Before we visited, I explained that Daddy's heart had stopped and that the doctors had hooked him up to a lot of machines to keep it beating properly. I also told them that he wouldn't be able to talk to them because the doctors had given him medicine that made him very sleepy. They asked if he could hear. I said I wasn't sure but just in case they should talk to him about their day.

They were hesitant when they walked into his room the first time, and curious about the beeping machines, but they weren't shocked or frightened. They jabbered away for a few minutes and then quickly got bored. I thought it best to keep the visit short, so after a few minutes I asked if they wanted to go for an ice cream.

Right from the start, my worst fear for Pat had always been that he was trapped inside his body. I worried that he was aware of his surroundings but unable to communicate his awareness to those around him. I couldn't imagine a more horrifying fate. The doctors assured me that if that were the case they'd be able to see much more brain activity, but their words were cold comfort. It didn't really matter what they said. I continued to believe he was in there somewhere.

As a result, I didn't behave any differently in his presence than I would have normally. Whenever I walked into his room I greeted him and asked about his day, then sat at his bedside and chatted to him about the kids. I read newspaper articles to him every day. When his *Sports Illustrated* came to the house, I brought it in and read stories to him from it as well.

I only got angry with him once. It happened at St. Mike's after the doctors informed me that we had to have a meeting. After they gave me his prognosis, I marched straight back to his room and really let him have it. I feared he was giving up or maybe already had. I feared he wasn't holding up his end of the bargain. "What are you doing?" I shrieked in a loud whisper. "You're not fighting hard enough. This is not the way this is supposed to end."

WHEN PAT WENT BACK to Joseph Brant, Hailey's pool party for her tenth birthday was only a few days away. Everyone told me to cancel the party. They thought I was crazy even to consider going through with it. But I refused. I was determined to normalize the kids' lives as much as possible. I didn't want my daughter's memory of her tenth birthday to be tainted by sadness and disappointment. I especially didn't want her to associate those feelings with her dad. The question in my mind then was never whether I'd go through with the party. The question was how I'd get through it.

Everybody was worried that I'd break down in the middle of the celebrations. That was definitely a worry, but oddly, it wasn't my biggest concern. My biggest worry was who was going to shoot the video. I obsessed about that. Pat had always been the videographer for family occasions. How could I possibly throw a party if he wasn't there to record it?

I realized that if I was determined to go through with the party, I was going to need help to bring it off. But that was problematic. Asking for help wasn't my strong suit. I was the planner, the party thrower. The only people I felt comfortable asking for help were my parents. But I didn't have any choice. I asked my brother Michael to shoot the video, my girlfriend Melanie to pick up the cake and my mom to organize the loot bags and balloons.

My next worry was how I was going to make it through the festivities without unravelling. I knew that if I allowed the image of Pat lying in a hospital bed hooked up to a ventilator to enter my mind during the proceedings I'd come undone. I had to lock up my feelings and throw away the key; otherwise, they'd engulf me.

I first discovered what a powerful tool compartmentalization could be after my dad died. The thought that he wouldn't be present to see me graduate made me unbearably sad. But I didn't want sadness to be my only memory of that day. I knew he wouldn't have wanted that for me either. To get through the day, I knew I had to force myself to set aside the awareness that he wasn't there. The sense of his absence shadowed me all day. I couldn't escape it entirely. But compartmentalizing my feelings helped me keep my grief at bay.

I knew the only way I'd get through Hailey's party was by tricking my brain into believing that Pat wasn't ill. So I decided to make up a story. I told myself the reason he couldn't make it to Hailey's party that year was because he was away on a business trip. The sleight of mind required to achieve that level of denial was far beyond any I'd ever achieved, even on my graduation day when my dad had passed away just prior, and I had real apprehensions about my ability to pull it off. However, experience had taught me that the only way I'd have a fighting chance of making it through that party was by convincing myself that I could. So I told myself that Hailey was going to have the best birthday party ever. Then I went around announcing my intentions to everyone else.

Miraculously, the strategy worked. For the first time since my life had shattered, I forgot my sorrow. For the first time since that terrible night, I felt like a human being again. It felt good to forget my troubles. It felt good to hear the joyful noise of kids splashing in the pool. It felt good to give my daughter the birthday memory she deserved. Making it through that birthday party was hugely emblematic for me. It inspired me to believe that if I could make it through those four hours, I could make it through anything.

CHAPTER FOUR

Above and Beyond

IN MAY 1991, with my grief over my father's death still raw, that awful final year of university behind me and a marketing degree in hand, I headed home to live with my mom and Ron and figure out the next chapter of my life. Fortunately they didn't charge me rent, and the insurance company where I'd worked summers in the accounting department had offered to keep me on that fall, so I had the luxury of taking my time to look for a job that would be a good fit for me and the right launchpad for my career. I decided to use that time to do some research.

I'd spent my first two years at university working towards a Bachelor of Applied Science with a major in consumer studies and a minor in consumer behaviour. After second year, the university introduced a Bachelor of Commerce in Marketing degree that still allowed me to major in marketing, but offered a much broader business background. I wanted a degree that would open up the most doors after graduation, so I switched programs after second year.

Marketing had long been a fascination of mine. I'd taken a few high school courses that had sparked my interest in the complicated variables that drove consumer behaviour — particularly those that inspired brand loyalty. By the time I'd graduated from university, I knew marketing was the path I wanted to pursue. I'd done well in my business courses, but marketing seemed like a more creative field, and one that offered the chance to connect directly with the consumer.

I also knew by then that I wanted to join a corporate marketing team and work on the client rather than agency side. A marketing department struck me as a truly dynamic place to work. It would expose me to the field's many diverse applications: research and product development, brand management, analytics, customer and market research, pricing, communications, advertising and public relations, and seemed to open up a world of limitless possibility.

That much was clear. But I had no idea where to apply or what companies might be interested in hiring me. So I began investigating my options. When I speak to young people who are setting out on their careers today, I talk a lot about the importance of research and preparation. I tell them thorough preparation will take any situation from good to great, and that you can never be too prepared. I tell my kids the same thing. But doing a thorough job takes time, and you have to be prepared to put in that time.

I know people who wing it, but I don't want to become one of those people. I think winging it is disrespectful to your audience. Besides, you can always tell who those people are. I can easily spot the ill-prepared candidates when I conduct interviews. They're the ones who get that deer-in-the-headlights look if I ask them a question they didn't anticipate.

In 1991, the internet was still in its infancy, so for the next few months, after work and on weekends, I spent hours at the library researching business publications to find the company that would be the best fit for me. I came across one that named the fifty best companies to work for in Canada. I read up on the creation stories, philosophies, histories, performance and growth records of several firms, made note of the ones that interested me, and winnowed down my list to my top three choices: Revlon, the global cosmetics brand; Dylex, one of the country's largest retail brands; and FedEx Express Canada, the global airline cargo company.

Of the three, FedEx Express Canada was my first choice. I knew I wanted to work for a brand with which I felt an emotional connection. I also knew that I wanted to work for a stellar company since marketing is all about the strength of the brand. Revlon and Dylex were top contenders, in part because of my interest in beauty and fashion and in part because of my familiarity with both brands. But FedEx Express Canada spoke to me in a way that the others did not. I also liked what I'd read about the founder of FedEx, the company's creation story and its people-first philosophy. I'd read an article about the company's philosophy that had made a strong impression on me. It talked about its P-S-P or People-Service-Profit motto. The idea was that if the company treated its people with trust and respect, they would go beyond what was expected of them in return for delivering exceptional service to its customers, and that exemplary service would result in profit for shareholders, thus allowing the company to reinvest in its people.

The books I'd read had talked about a career as a journey and the necessity of having a passion for that journey, rather than viewing your place of employment simply as a place to clock in every day and collect a paycheque. I certainly didn't have a passion for transporting packages. But I liked the sound of the P-S-P philosophy and the brand's people-first approach deeply resonated with me.

When I was looking for work, none of the companies on my list was advertising for entry-level positions. When you're in the market for a job, that's almost always the case. I didn't know anything about company hiring procedures then. If I hadn't done a deep research dive, I might not have bothered to apply. It was only through my reading that I learned circumstances changed at companies all the time and managers stockpiled résumés to fill vacant positions. I didn't wait to be asked. I applied.

People often ask me the secret of my success. When I

tell them I think one of the main reasons I've succeeded is because I go beyond what's expected of me, they look at me as if to say *That's it? That's your big secret?* They think I have some magic formula. But there isn't any magic formula. You just have to go the extra mile every day.

When I was fifteen I had a part-time job as a birthday hostess at Chuck E. Cheese's, a family event and entertainment centre. From the moment I was hired I made up my mind to become the best birthday hostess the company had ever seen.

When I was a hostess, I used to watch the supervisors and wonder how I'd improve matters if I were in their role. No one told me to do this. I simply had ambitions to move up, so I imagined myself at the next level and began to think and act as if I already had the position. I was careful not to usurp anyone else's role. I simply demonstrated my willingness and ability to handle more responsibility by pitching in wherever I saw the need.

Organizing came easily to me — I had a knack for multi-tasking and seeing the big picture, so I kept an eye out to see where I could lend a hand. (On my kindergarten report card, my teacher described me as her little class helper.) If I noticed that, despite trying their best, some of the other hostesses were struggling to stay on top of their tables, I helped out. Maybe one table needed a bill, another pop and a third tokens for the arcade. Instead of making three trips, I grabbed everything at once and made one. In a little over a year, I was offered a supervisor role. Later on in high school I worked as a sales clerk at Fairweather, a women's clothing store. Again I pictured myself in a supervisory position and contributed in a supportive way. Again I was promoted.

I always loved a challenge and I was always willing to push myself to be the best that I could be. But it wasn't until my high school jobs that I realized there was another factor in the mix, and it seemed to have almost magical powers. If I wanted to succeed, all I had to do was visualize my goals and work towards them with laser-like focus. As long as I focused on my destination and didn't worry about my path, I could accomplish whatever I wanted. If I just kept determining what baby steps I could take towards my goals, arriving would be a matter of time, not debate.

I make a point of trying to exceed expectations in whatever I do. I go that route partly because I was taught that you only get out of something what you put into it. But I also do it because I believe putting in extra effort takes you to your destination faster and improves your chances of winding up in the right place. Some people think it takes too much time to make the extra effort, but I think that's a shortsighted view. Going above and beyond will always deliver the best return on your investment.

When I was compiling my short list of companies to approach, I came across articles that recommended I target my application package to the needs of individual employers. I compiled three separate versions of my résumé, highlighting my skills, talents, educational background and work experience differently in each case. It took more time to craft three tailored résumés, but I was marketing myself and I'd learned in school that one of the most fundamental rules of marketing was demonstrating an understanding of my audience's needs.

To put it another way, I was trying to catch a fish. Wouldn't I have a better chance if I used the right lure? You need to put yourself in the position of the person who'll be looking at what you send in. I often receive proposals from people who want to forge a business partnership with our company. You'd be surprised at how many send their proposals via Purolator or UPS. You want to do business with FedEx Express Canada and you send me your package with our competition? I don't think my assistant even bothers to give me those anymore.

When I applied, my goal was to distinguish myself from the other applicants. I figured if I mailed in my résumés they'd just languish in a pile on someone's desk and I'd remain a faceless name. If I hand-delivered them, however, I'd demonstrate my initiative and enthusiasm, and possibly get the chance to make a personal connection with someone on staff. And so I decided to drop mine off in person.

I know the internet has transformed the way people seek employment today, but I firmly believe that the fundamental principles for catching an employer's eye remain the same, and that making a polished first impression will never go out of style. When I hired, I saw a lot of packages riddled with typos and grammatical errors. The applicants hadn't even bothered to use a spell-check program. Anyone can make mistakes, of course, but, again, think about your package from the employer's point of view. If you're that careless when you're trying to land the job, why on earth would they think you'd be more thorough once you'd landed it?

Many companies will only allow you to apply digitally today. Even so, you still have to find a way to make your application stand out. I believe there's always a way to make a personal connection — and, today, technology's dehumanizing influence has made it even more important to make those connections.

Your cover letter is your best chance to make one. Most of the cover letters I've read during my career have been generic. Many applicants simply recapped the highlights of their business career, but if I wanted that information, all I had to do was turn the page and read their résumés. Your cover letter is valuable real estate. Why waste it?

Business skills are important, of course, but the letters that piqued my interest most and made me feel that I had to take the time to meet the individuals who wrote them were the ones that gave me a sense of the person and their passions. Maybe they loved going skiing with their family. Maybe they worked with a rescue organization. Maybe they'd taken a career detour at some point to broaden their horizons and re-evaluate their life goals. You only have a couple of paragraphs to make an impression. Use them wisely.

My résumé polished, I turned my attention to refining my personal presentation. I've always been acutely aware that perception is reality, so the day I dropped off my résumé I wanted anyone I met to assume that I already worked at the company. Accordingly, I dressed the part: pinstripe suit, pumps, hair neatly pulled back. By the time

I walked through the tall glass doors of FedEx Express Canada's then-headquarters in Mississauga, Ontario, I was thoroughly prepared and I'd made a series of conscious choices to ensure I'd be taken seriously.

Two things immediately caught my notice that day: the striking, massive brand logo, and all the people buzzing back and forth through reception. The sense of energy was electric. I imagined myself talking business with my colleagues. I knew instantly, and with every fibre of my being, that this was the place I wanted to be. I went to the front desk and told the receptionist that I wanted to speak to the marketing director's assistant, referring to the director by name. I knew the name because I'd called beforehand to say I was preparing a package for the director and needed to know it.

By having that information at hand, I conveyed that I was in the know and increased my chances that the receptionist would call the director's assistant out to reception — which she did. More importantly, when I strode to the front desk I exuded confidence. Not that I wasn't nervous. I was. But the feeling was more excitement than anxiety. I had confidence because I'd done my homework.

When the assistant came out, I introduced myself, said I'd just graduated with a marketing degree, admired the company's philosophy, would love to work there one day, and asked if I could leave my résumé with her. Then, because she seemed to be the sort of person who'd understand what it was like to be in my shoes, I chatted her up a bit. I didn't try to ingratiate myself and I didn't overstay my welcome. I just tried to be warm and personable.

The next day I sent her flowers and a personal thank-you note. I'm not saying that you have to open an account with a florist to get your foot in the door. I am saying that you should follow up in a memorable way. After I was hired, I learned that shortly after I'd dropped off my résumé the director came out of her office and told her assistant that she'd just received approval to hire another person in the marketing department. She had a stack of résumés sitting on her desk. Mine was on top. "Boy," she told her boss, "have I got someone for you."

Sending a handwritten note by traditional mail may sound old school, but that's precisely why it will make an impression. It will stand out from the blizzard of texts and emails everybody receives these days. Above all, though, a personal note demonstrates your willingness to do more than what is expected of you. That's another message that never gets old.

A FEW WEEKS LATER, I received a call to come in for an interview. After I got that call, I didn't put my feet up. I put my foot on the gas. I gave myself a refresher course on the company's history and philosophy, pored over Statistics Canada reports to bone up on industry trends and read books about how to stand out in an interview. I picked up a motherlode of tips: to listen intently and answer concisely, to ask for a moment to collect my thoughts if I needed time before answering, to make eye contact, avoid fidgeting and breathe. I learned that it was a good idea to think up a few questions of my own to ask the interviewer, as long as I couldn't have found the answers elsewhere. (I planned to ask the manager what she loved most about her job and what she considered its greatest challenges.) I also picked up that I should anticipate the questions I might be asked and rehearse my answers — not to sound scripted, but to speak with authority.

As I walked towards the boardroom on interview day, I kept thinking that I had sixty minutes to make the most memorable impression of my life. I don't recall the manager's questions. I just remember how effortless it all felt and having the sense that I could handle whatever she threw at me.

I was standing in my parents' kitchen a few days later when the call came. It was the manager on the line. "You did a fantastic job," she said. "You'd be a great fit for our team. We'd love to offer you a position. How soon can you start?"

I could barely contain my glee. I had a title: associate marketing specialist. I had a starting salary: $28,500. It was my first grown-up job where I'd have the chance to use my marketing degree. And it wasn't just any old entry-level position. It was my dream job. It had taken me five months of preparation to place myself in the path of opportunity, but I'd landed exactly where I wanted to be.

My career had officially begun. I was twenty-two years old.

AFTER GRADUATION, Pat had set his sights on a career in the construction industry. He had taken a job at the building supply company in Burlington where he'd worked part-time in the yard and behind the counter during high school and college. By the time I graduated, he'd been working there for a year. Now both gainfully employed, we hurled ourselves into our careers.

My first day at FedEx Express Canada I was so excited to go to work I showed up at the office before eight a.m. Around nine, the assistant who'd taken my résumé gave me a tour and showed me to my cubicle. A few minutes later my manager came by to welcome me, say a few agencies were pitching that day, hand me an agency brief and ask me to sit in and help pick our new agency of record.

My heart sank. I thought I'd be reviewing paperwork on my first day. If I'd known I'd be evaluating agency pitches, I'd have read up on how to critique one. But preparing was out of the question. On the way to the boardroom, I told myself, Lisa, you're the rookie. Your job is to listen, learn and be ready to offer an opinion if you're asked for one. If you are asked, whatever you do don't ramble on. Keep your answer short and sweet. (I'd picked that tip up in the books I'd read on how to shine in an interview.)

The director, manager and I sat on one side of the boardroom table. The pitch teams came in one by one and pitched us. After each team had left the room, we discussed the pitch and the director asked for my opinion. I did my best to offer useful insights in a non-controversial way. After we'd finished critiquing all three, the director asked me what agency I'd pick as my first choice, why I'd chosen that agency and why I saw myself working with their team. I was worried I'd choose an agency that nobody else wanted to work with. To my relief, we all ended up picking the same agency that day.

I was giddy on my way home from work that day. It was only my first day and I'd already had an experience that I'd only read about in books. It was scary to be tossed into the deep end, but I later came to realize it was the most valuable learning experience my manager could have given me. I've been thrown into the deep end many times since then, and I longed for a life jacket every time. Unfortunately, life doesn't always work that way.

CHAPTER FIVE

Operation Miracle

ONCE ST. MIKE'S SENT PAT BACK to Joseph Brant in the second week after his heart attack, I wanted to know the strategy the doctors had mapped out to help him recover. So as soon as he was settled in the ICU, I asked them to tell me their plan for bringing him back. However, it quickly became apparent that the doctors there were focused on keeping him alive. As a result, their involvement with him consisted mostly of popping by to check his condition and give him his meds. It also became apparent that they were all focused on their individual roles. The cardiologist was worrying about his heart. The neurologist was worrying about his brain. The nutritionist was worrying about his feeding tube. Nobody was looking at the big picture.

Patrick wasn't the only person to whom the doctors were prescribing meds. My GP wanted to put me on anti-depressants. I said no. I feared that taking medication would cloud my mind. If I wanted to make sure that Pat had every conceivable chance of recovering, I had to manage his care, and for that, I had to be fully alert.

At one point, the hospital assigned me a social worker whose job was to ensure that I didn't sink into a deep depression. I'm sure she meant well, but when she began speaking to me in pitying tones and treating me like a feeble, barely coping victim, it was the last thing I needed.

I needed to feel positive and in control. Ever since Pat had taken ill, I'd been overwhelmed by profound feelings of helplessness at not having had any control over his fate. Taking a proactive role in his care allowed me to feel that I still had some agency in the matter. If I couldn't prevent what had happened to him, then at least I might be able to exercise some influence over the outcome. My preferred therapy was to spend my days engaging in front-line care management and my nights on the computer digging up any information I could find about heart attacks and brain trauma.

Researching was the only place I found any release. Just as I'd pored over business journals to help me make an informed career choice, I returned from the hospital around nine, read medical journals online until midnight or one in the morning and functioned on four or five hours of sleep a night to find the information I needed to help Pat recover. I tracked down relevant studies, read the abstracts and paid a fee to read the entire study when required. I printed out papers of interest, highlighted key sections and made copious notes. Often the medical jargon was confusing, so I googled words I didn't understand. Sometimes I had to read the studies a dozen times to grasp their meaning. Eventually I became so conversant with the terminology that the cardiologist asked me if I had a medical background.

The more I read, the more questions I had about Pat's treatment, so I compiled a list of queries and started hitting the staff with tough questions whenever I saw them. Pat was on a ton of drugs. I researched every one. At one point the doctors put him on a new medication and he started having seizures. I researched the new drug to see if it might be causing the problem and I raised my concerns with the doctors. If I suggested they try a new drug or treatment and they said that it couldn't be done, I asked them why not, then hammered them with facts. I always made sure I was well armed with evidence before I asked.

At first when the neurologist saw me in the hallway, I had so many questions for him that I'm sure he wanted to run when he saw me coming. But I didn't care. Passivity was not an option. If even the slightest chance existed for me to uncover information that could help Pat, I had to track it down. I had to leave no stone unturned. When the doctors couldn't offer me any medical solutions, I tried alternative therapies. I followed every lead down every dark alley.

Eventually I became so knowledgeable that I requested and ran a few meetings with the neurologist, cardiologist and nutritionist. I wanted to gather all the professionals together in the same room so they could talk to each other. I ran the meetings like business meetings. I went in with an agenda, pressed the staff for better communication around the drugs they were prescribing and stayed on top of them to ensure they were keeping abreast of the latest research.

Since Pat had fallen ill, I'd been plagued with questions about what had caused his cardiac arrest. Nobody could give me an answer. I knew that he had a family history of heart disease. His grandfather had dropped dead of a heart attack at forty-seven and his dad had had two triple bypass surgeries. I assumed that clogged arteries had been the culprit. But I didn't know for sure.

The question nagged at me because apart from his smoking (which, other than his travel schedule, was the only serious issue we ever fought about), Pat took good care of himself. He was in such great shape that when the firemen who tried to revive him laid eyes on him that night they thought he was one of their own. We both had annual physicals in Toronto at one of the country's top executive healthcare clinics. Pat had earned top marks at his last checkup. How was it possible that the experts had missed such a ticking time bomb?

I was concerned that if he had another heart attack it would kill him. And if genetics had played a role, I was terrified that one of the kids would be next. I told the doctors I had to know what had caused his heart attack

and pressed them to send him to Hamilton General —
now Hamilton Health Sciences — for an implantable
cardioverter-defibrillator (ICD). If his heart stopped
again, I'd at least have the assurance that it would shock it
back to a normal rhythm. Eventually the doctors agreed
to send Pat for the procedure.

The doctor who performed the procedure found that
Pat's arteries were pristine, and suggested doing DNA
testing to see if his heart attack had a genetic cause.
I learned that the Mayo Clinic had excellent genetic
testing facilities, so, at my request, he arranged to have
Pat's blood sent to the Mayo Clinic for testing. When the
results came back, he informed me that Pat had a condition known as Long QT Syndrome Type 6. There was a
fifty percent chance that gene could be passed on to the
kids and he advised me to have their blood tested. When
I heard those words, my heart stopped. What was I in for
next? I had the kids' blood taken immediately and sent for
testing. Then I waited.

DURING THOSE MONTHS AT JOE BRANT, I'd also been
investigating Pat's rehab options. My mom and I had visited a few facilities, but none would admit him. His prognosis was too poor. In the course of my investigations,
I'd found a program for severely brain-injured patients
at Chedoke Hospital in Hamilton. (It, too, is now part
of Hamilton Health Sciences.) By every measure, the
program was ideal. The team specialized in working
with non-responsive, slow-to-recover patients, and the

hospital was within commuting distance, but Pat's chances of being accepted were borderline at best. So in mid-October, when I received a call that the team was going to send out someone to assess him, I was elated. It was my first glimmer of hope in months. At the same time, I was terrified he wouldn't qualify.

Pat's entire future was riding on that assessment. And I was facing the interview of my life. I was powerless to control his responses, but I knew that I had control over mine. So I thought long and hard about the best way to handle myself during that assessment.

My instinct was to push the assessor hard to admit Pat. But if I became confrontational, or worse, started behaving like a hysterical wife, I knew it would be game over. I had to remain calm; otherwise the assessor would report back to the team that on top of dealing with a severely disabled patient they'd have a crazy person on their hands.

I knew I needed a strategy going into that interview, so I thought about how I'd strategize in a business setting. Before an important meeting at work, I always tried to have sidebar meetings to get a sense of the questions that were likely to arise and prepare my answers ahead of time. When I had to make a presentation, I usually rehearsed dozens of times to make sure my delivery felt as natural as breathing. I had no way of knowing what the assessor would ask, but I thought deeply about what I'd say to help him see Pat as a human being and not just another case on his roster. And I rehearsed my breathing techniques to make sure I'd maintain my composure.

The assessor was in his twenties. As soon as he walked

into Pat's room, I said, "Hi, I'm Lisa. This is my husband, Patrick." I immediately launched into a story about how we'd met in grade nine, were high school sweethearts and had four kids. Hailey, our eldest, had just had her tenth birthday, and next came Chloe, who was seven, then Mya and Jack, who were five and three.

He listened patiently. When I was finished, he explained that he had a checklist of tests to go through to evaluate Pat's level of responsiveness. He said the team was looking for some kind of response, however minimal. Once he'd completed the assessment, he'd report back to the team and they'd meet to determine whether to admit him.

He stood on one side of Pat and I stood on the other. He started going down his checklist: "Pat, can you squeeze my hand? Pat, can you hear me? If you can understand me, blink one for yes and two for no. Okay, now I want you to track my pen with your eyes." He went through all the items on his list. Pat didn't respond. I was stoic. It took every ounce of self-control I had not to break down.

He told me in a neutral tone that Pat was on the cusp for admittance. He said someone would be in touch with me in the next couple of weeks, and then he turned to leave. Before he walked out, I wanted to give him something to take back to the team, something to make them feel that even though Pat was on the borderline it would be worth taking a shot on him. I knew from my research that some families abandoned patients with severe brain injuries and strong family support was one of the program's admittance criteria. I wanted the assessor to know that abandonment wasn't going to be an issue in this case.

As he was on his way out, I said, "Just so you know, this is only a temporary setback. He's not a quitter. He's going to pull through."

For the next ten days, I waited. At the end of October, I received a call from Esther McEvoy. She was calling from the Acquired Brain Injury Program at Chedoke Hospital. She told me the team had decided to admit Pat. They'd be coming to pick him up in a couple of days.

CHAPTER SIX

You're in Charge of You

IN 1992, SOON AFTER I LANDED MY FEDEX JOB, Pat wanted us to move in together. Several of our couple friends were already doing so, and he didn't see any reason why we should wait. But I was more of a long-range thinker than Patrick, and I argued that while couples often lived together before marriage to see if they were compatible, we had that one covered. Why not continue living at home for a couple of years and save for a house? Still, as practical as I was about such matters, I was also a romantic: the other reason I wanted to wait was because I envisioned him proposing and carrying me over the threshold of our new home after our honeymoon.

In the early fall of 1993, I started to get antsy about when Pat was going to ask me to marry him. "What's taking him so long?" I asked my friends. "Why doesn't he propose already?" My impatience wasn't helping matters. Then one night he suggested that we go out for a nice dinner. When he picked me up at my parents' house I could tell he was nervous. Okay, I thought. Tonight's the night.

He took me to a fancy restaurant and we ordered drinks. After we'd ordered, he asked what kind of diamond I'd like for an engagement ring. My heart sank. It wasn't exactly the question I'd been hoping to hear. Tonight clearly wasn't going to be the night.

"I prefer square or emerald cut to round."

"Like this?" he asked, as he pulled out a small box, which he opened to reveal a beautiful emerald-cut diamond ring.

Then he got down on one knee. "Lisa, will you marry me?" he asked.

I burst into tears. "Yes!" I replied, my mascara running. "A million times yes!"

We set a tentative wedding date for the spring of 1994. Patrick told me he wanted to start a family as soon as we got married, but again I argued for waiting. My theory was that we'd never be that free again. Why not enjoy that time while it was ours and create a few memories as a married couple before the onslaught began? Again, he deferred to my wishes. He always let me make the big decisions. He went along with me partly because he admired my ability to see the big picture, but also because he trusted my judgment and knew I had our best interests at heart.

Except for my grief over losing my dad, life was unfolding exactly as I imagined it would. Then, in October 1993, a month after our engagement, Pat's mom was diagnosed with brain cancer and was told she had less than a year to live. It didn't seem possible that history was repeating itself. But it was.

It was hard enough seeing one parent felled by the disease. But two? How could that be? Pat had been at my side through my dad's final months. Now the roles were reversed. We'd seen how quickly my dad had deteriorated. We knew his mom didn't have much time. We moved up our date so she could dance with her son on his wedding day. We were married in January. She died in May.

That summer I was still processing my grief when I received a call that my brother Bradley, who was fourteen, had been hit by a car while he was out riding his bike. He had to have part of his skull removed to address the bleeding on his brain and the doctors put him into a medically induced coma to bring down the brain swelling. He lay unconscious for two days before he awoke. Miraculously, he didn't have brain damage. And then eight months later, I received word that my best friend Melanie's sister, Alayne, had been murdered.

The three of us had been friends since high school. I had attended Alayne's wedding. The marriage didn't work out. She'd just left her husband. We'd helped her move out two days earlier. She went back to the house with a friend the next day to pick up a few things when she thought her husband would be at work. He wasn't at work. He was home, waiting for her with a hunting rifle. He chased her down the driveway and shot her. Then he turned the gun on himself.

There are no words to describe how devastated I was. I couldn't believe her life was over. How she'd never have kids. Never grow old. I couldn't get the image of her running for her life down that driveway out of my mind. Watching my father slip away was hard. But seeing my friend's life brutally taken from her in that way was almost too much to bear.

In the space of five years I went from graduating, landing my dream job, marrying my high school sweetheart, buying our first home together, wondering whether my kid brother would emerge from a coma, winning a promotion to department manager and burying three people who had been incredibly close to me.

Death has a way of clarifying life. When your life is all shiny with possibility and then it suddenly takes a hard right turn and you slam headlong into its fragility, the experience focuses you — especially when you're so young. It definitely focused me. After so much calamity and loss I vowed to live my life to the fullest each and every day. I understood in a way that I didn't before that life can change in a heartbeat. I only had so much time on this planet and I had to spend it judiciously. I could not waste a moment. I had to focus only on what mattered.

Family was what mattered to Pat and me. He and I had both grown up in large families, and we both wanted a lot of kids. So a year after I became a manager we had our first child. Hailey had my fair skin, Pat's features and dark hair. She also had colic. For the first few months she cried all night. Pat couldn't even take a shift since I was nursing. She slept during the day, but people kept dropping by with gifts then. My mom spelled me a bit, but sometimes days went by before I had the chance to shower. Managing to bathe was my greatest feat.

It didn't take me long to figure out that going to work was a breeze compared to caring for a child. I kept wondering why nobody had prepared me for motherhood. I couldn't fathom why anyone would choose to have more than one child. If this was a preview of what was in store, I told everyone I'd never have another. After three months, the colic went away. The first time Hailey slept during the night I felt as if I'd spent a month at Canyon Ranch spa. For the next few weeks, I got some R&R. Then I got bored.

I'd worked right up until two days before going into labour, and I'd told my boss I planned to take the standard paid six-month maternity leave. But being out of the loop was driving me crazy. By the four-month mark, I started to get antsy. I kept calling the office to check in. Do we have numbers on our outdoor campaign yet? How's the direct mail blitz going?

I know some working moms who are miserable not being home with their kids. I know others who enjoy working but stay home because they believe it's the right thing to do. They plan to return to the workforce when their kids are older. I think it is important to do what is right for you, what makes you happy. As long as parents are happy, the children will be happy. For me, staying home had never crossed my mind.

I loved my work. I found it challenging, creatively nurturing and absolutely central to my identity. I also wanted a family, and it had never occurred to me that I couldn't have both. So whether I'd return to work was never in question. The only question was when. I found a daycare five minutes from our house and went back in January.

THE STORY OF MY CAREER has been the story of one long, never-ending process of self-education. I didn't wait to be taught. I taught myself. If knowledge is power, then knowledge has certainly been a wellspring of power for me. Learning doesn't just nourish my curiosity and broaden my understanding. Learning calms me. The more knowledge I have, the more in control I feel. If there's a better cure for anxiety, I've never found it.

Whenever I have to learn something, I start with reading. I give myself an immersion course every time I have to take on a new assignment. Reading gives me the lay of the land. I did it when I was trying to launch my career. I did it when I was preparing for my first interview. I did it every time I was promoted.

I read on and off as a child, but I didn't start reading in a serious way until I started taking business courses in high school and developed a fascination with the psychological side of consumer behaviour. At the time, a lot of girls my age were into reading fiction and romance novels, but I was more drawn to books that offered me practical information. So even before I knew what career path I intended to follow, I was reading business and self-help books.

The moment I was hired, I became a sponge. When I found out that I'd be working on ad campaigns, I made it my mission to learn as much as I could about my new world. I'd taken a couple of university courses in advertising, so I started by digging out my notes to refresh my memory. I devoured books on the subject so I could master the industry jargon and speak with authority in meetings. Value proposition, brand attributes, executional considerations: I learned it all. After the first few meetings, my boss told me I had the lingo of someone who'd been working in the industry for ten years.

Once I became a manager, I made another bee-line for the bookstore — this time for a crash course in Management 101. Again, my goal was to soak up as much information as I could. If reading couldn't provide all the answers, it could at least point me in the direction of the questions I needed to ask.

When I was appointed VP sales, I had to lead a sales force that lived or died by the deal. At the time, I knew exactly one thing about negotiating: you had to start at a higher price and negotiate down. The day I got the job I stopped at the bookstore on my way home from work, headed for the section on sales strategies and negotiating skills and basically stripped the shelves. Then I went home, made dinner, put the kids to bed and started reading. Among other things, I discovered that you had to know your bottom line going into the negotiation so you knew when to walk away, and both parties had to emerge feeling like winners for the deal to be successful and the relationship sustainable. This was laughably rudimentary stuff, but at least I picked up a few basic principles, and the more I read, the more I calmed down. Once I started to rise through the ranks, a mentor advised me to broaden the scope of my reading and stay up-to-date on global industry and market trends. According to him, it wasn't just a good way to expand my knowledge. It was a useful networking tool. If I crossed paths with a superior, I'd be able to opine with authority on matters outside of Canada. I took his advice. I broadened my reading.

Once I had my foot in the door, I moved up quickly: three rungs in four years. I spent one year at entry level, two as a marketing specialist and one-and-a-half as a senior marketing specialist. Next was the manager's job. By the time it came into view, I knew I wanted to run my own team, so I asked my mentors the best way to proceed. They gave me two critical pieces of advice. First, I should make my intentions known to my manager and director (but not before excelling at my current job). Second, I should put myself forward for lateral promotions whenever I could.

I followed their advice, which turned out to be solid. When my manager left, I was promoted to manager. Two years later I had the opportunity to make a lateral move. I took it. After a year I became a director. A few years later I was appointed VP. A few years after that I was offered another lateral position. I took that one, too. Four years later I was appointed president. I went from entry-level to president in eighteen years.

After I had my foot in the door, I didn't think okay, now I'm going to spend the next eighteen years moving packages around and when I'm forty-one years old I'm going to become the first female and the first Canadian president of the company, and I'm going to realize my ambitions after having four kids and deal with a devastating life crisis. If anyone had told me that that's what my story was going to be I'd have told them they were crazy. I didn't have a master plan. I just had the desire to keep growing. So, I kept pushing myself and taking baby steps towards my goals so they wouldn't feel so daunting. As soon as I landed at one level, I looked to the next.

Whenever a new opportunity presented itself, I was faced with a choice. Do I stay where I am? Or do I take a chance and grow? Every time I chose to grow. (The only opportunities I turned down would have necessitated me moving to head office in Memphis. I declined because I wasn't prepared to take Pat away from a career he loved or lose the proximity of my family's support.) Otherwise, I took whatever opportunities came my way. Even when the job terrified me, I never shied away. Every time, I said bring it on.

One of the most important skills anyone can learn regardless of their role in the company — whether a junior employee or a CEO — is how to listen. From my first day at work I paid close attention to how my colleagues conducted themselves in meetings and observed the dynamics that played out in the room as a result. I didn't just find those interactions instructional, although they were certainly that. I found them endlessly fascinating. And by keeping my eyes open I made an important discovery: most people have something to teach you whether they mean to teach it to you or not.

Observation became my ticket to understanding my new environment. It taught me the kind of person I wanted to be in the workplace and the kind of person I definitely did not want to be. It taught me the value of becoming a good listener and a team player. But I didn't just observe my colleagues. I observed how my manager coached me. I noticed how she spoke to me, encouraged me to ask questions and advise her if I needed anything. I also paid close attention to other managers' leadership styles. I watched how they handled situations and reflected on how I'd behave in similar circumstances. I didn't obsess about any of this. I simply paid attention and thought about how I'd behave if I were in charge, just as I had during my high school jobs.

I took particular interest in how different individuals handled confrontational situations. Early on, I remember one manager who never let anyone finish a sentence. He constantly interrupted them and made them feel that what they had to say was so irrelevant that it wasn't even worth letting them finish. I decided then and there that if I ever became a manager I would always let others have a voice.

When I was a director, sometimes I had to make presentations to the president and VPs. On such occasions, the view from the podium was particularly instructive. Naturally, I was nervous when I had to present, so if I looked around the room and saw someone making eye contact and encouraging me with nods and smiles, I was deeply appreciative of their silent encouragement and I vowed I would do the same for others.

Before long, I started putting all my observations to strategic use. I became adept at reading body language. It's amazing what you can pick up just by reading someone's body language. I learned to take those cues very seriously — more seriously, in fact, that what the person was actually saying. I became especially proficient at reading my bosses' body language and using that knowledge to gauge their state of mind. The skill came in handy if I wanted to avoid having to meet with one of them on a day when they weren't in the best mood. Fortunately I've always reported to bosses I admired, but everybody has bad days.

I KNOW OF WOMEN who complain bitterly that they can't advance beyond a certain level in their careers. Even though they're just as qualified as men — and sometimes more qualified — no matter how hard they try, they can't break into the boys' club. I understand those women's frustrations, but I don't share them. My experience as a woman in a man's world has been different than theirs. Not only did men not stand in my way — they were instrumental in helping me advance.

With one exception, I've reported to men throughout my career. Many were my mentors. They guided me practically and philosophically, served as my sounding board, sponsored me for pivotal opportunities, connected me to the right people, saw talents in me I didn't know I had and showed confidence in me when I lacked it in myself.

I consider them all to be collaborators in my success. What's more, they didn't just point me in the right direction; often they handed me the GPS.

When I was still very junior, one of my male mentors told me that whenever I crossed paths with someone senior to me in the hallway, cafeteria, elevator or at a work event, I should use that time wisely to make an impression, even if that person wasn't in my chain of command. He said that if I were up for a promotion the decision maker wouldn't just evaluate my technical leadership skills; he'd give equal weight to how seamlessly I'd mesh with the team, and those casual encounters were one of the best ways for me to make an impression. At the same time, he cautioned me about taking an understated approach when I had those conversations. The point was to make a connection, not ambush the person and jam information down their throat.

So whenever I bumped into senior people, I made an effort to chat with them intelligently about business or current events. I might mention an article I thought would interest them and offer to send it to them. Then I followed up.

If I hadn't been handed that advice early in my career, I'm fairly sure I'd have done my best to make emotional connections whenever I had the chance, but I probably wouldn't have viewed those interactions as mini-interviews. Taking a strategic approach to those exchanges definitely advanced my career. After I was appointed president, I learned that all of the people with whom I'd been having those conversations over the years had told my boss I'd do a great job. Never underestimate the power of interviewing in the elevator.

When I meet someone, whether it's in a professional or social setting, I have three rules. I make eye contact. I try to draw them out. And I listen carefully to what they say. I really try to listen deeply. Most people, I've found, just want to be heard — even though many are terrible listeners. Fortunately, I had an early mentor who schooled me in the importance of listening: my dad. "You have two ears and one mouth for a reason," he used to say. I think about his words all the time.

Good listeners have curiosity and empathy. They know how to make others feel valued and put them at ease. They do it by demonstrating that others are worth listening to. But even if they don't find what the person is saying all that fascinating, they never let on, because good listeners have manners. Poor listeners, on the other hand, don't listen so much as lie in wait or look for an opening to hijack the conversation and steer it back to their favourite topic: themselves. I think we've all had to suffer those types.

WHEN I FIRST BECAME a manager, I wanted my staff to know that while we worked as a team, I also cared about them as individuals. I believed that if I established an emotional bond with my staff, I'd make them feel valued as individuals, and if they felt valued as individuals they'd achieve more as a team. I genuinely like people and have a natural curiosity about them, so showing an interest in my staff wasn't an act. Besides, I firmly believe that if my interest had been insincere they'd have sensed my insincerity in a nanosecond.

I made a conscious effort to get out of my office and connect with my team. I inquired about their lives outside of the office. I asked about their weekends, their kids, their big news. The more curiosity I showed in them, the more they shared with me about their lives. I was careful not to probe or violate boundaries. I just wanted them to see that that I was making an effort to get to know the person behind the employee ID and that we didn't have to talk shop all the time.

Some people love to chat about their personal lives while others are all business, so I had to learn what kind of person I was dealing with. It has to do with the idea of situational leadership: understanding that people are different and have different working styles, and adjusting your leadership approach accordingly. But even when people aren't inclined to share, I've found that most like to feel that you're taking an interest in them.

Attitude is a crucial variable in your success — much more so than many people realize. It communicates who you are and signals to others what to expect from you. That's why it's so important to become aware of the mood you're projecting. I believe you can choose your state of mind in much the same way that you choose your outfit every day.

I'm not suggesting you can simply will away a clinical depression. Nor am I saying that you're not allowed to have down days. I just think it's important to think of your attitude as your calling card. Or, to put it in today's terms: your personal brand. The first step in controlling your mood is knowing the kind of mood you're in. It all comes back to self-awareness. You have to be conscious to make conscious choices.

When I was a director, I had to deal with a manager who was in a perpetually grumpy mood. He snapped at others for no good reason and had a habit of projecting his misery at everyone around him. His carriage and body language were so distancing that people were actually afraid of him. One day I asked him a simple question and he practically tore my head off. I was almost back at my office when I decided that enough was enough. I turned around, went back to his office and called him out on his behaviour. "You know what?" I said. "I'm really sorry that you're having a bad day, but all I did was ask you a simple question. There was no need to bite my head off. I don't know what's going on in your life, but that was uncalled for." He was genuinely taken aback at my reaction and sincerely apologized for his behaviour. But his response told me that he had no idea how much negativity he was spewing, let alone how his prickliness was affecting others.

So, as I did with my other colleagues, I began taking an interest in his life, and he started to open up to me. His body language changed completely and he turned out to be a real softie. I realized his prickliness was just a defence he'd developed to keep others at a distance, and I had a lot more empathy for him after I'd gained that insight. But I'd never have gained it unless I'd made the effort to connect with him.

My other mission as a manager was to let my team know that while we were there to do a job, we didn't have to be serious all the time. We spend so much time at the office — I think work should be fun, too. So I encouraged my team to play baseball against some of the other departments, held strategy sessions at my home and initiated team-building activities.

When I became a vice-president, I put so much thought into planning fun events for my sales teams that one of my reps nicknamed me the VP of Fun. (Planning fun events is not a chore for me. I love throwing parties. If I ever need a fallback, I'll go into event planning.)

To this day, I'm always up for a little levity at work. Every September, we hold a tailgate party at head office to kick off NFL season. One year, one of the teams brought in electric scooters for the event. I hopped on and began driving around the parking lot, much to the consternation of my VP legal, who begged me to at least remove my three-inch heels.

UNTIL I BECAME A MANAGER, I could rely on the tools I had in my toolkit to keep advancing. However, once I reached the managerial level, I needed new skills to do my job and I realized the only way I was going to acquire them was by training myself to develop the skills I lacked.

People are often surprised when I say this. They think successful leaders are born with all the traits they need to become successful. But that's rarely the case. Usually they're born with some of the skills they require and they have to pick up others along the way. For instance, if you aspire to become a leader, it probably helps to be a people person, since you have to interact with people all the time. But we can't all be gifted air-fillers. Indeed, many leaders are introverted and shy. If they are, they have to find some way to adapt.

Former Yahoo CEO Marissa Mayer has said that she was so shy that for the first fifteen minutes of any party, including one in her own home, she wanted to flee. To resist the urge, she looked at her watch and told herself that she couldn't leave until "time x," and if she was still having a terrible time at "x," she could leave. If she forced herself to stay for a fixed period, she often found that she overcame her social awkwardness and actually started having fun.

I don't suffer from shyness. I suffer from a lack of patience. I also have a tendency to talk too fast. When I first became a manager, the words tumbled out of me so quickly that nobody had a clue what I was saying. Either people constantly asked me to repeat myself or they gave me quizzical looks.

I'm also inclined to make decisions quickly and then I expect others to keep up with me. When I was one person on a team, none of these traits was problematic. Then, I could work at my own pace, since I only had myself to consider. But once I was put in charge of a team, I had to slow down; otherwise, I'd leave people behind. That's when I first became familiar with the concept of situational leadership I mentioned earlier: the necessity of managing different people in different ways. If I expected everyone around me to work at warp speed, my pace might suit those with aggressive goals who enjoyed being pushed, but I'd lose the ones who didn't like working that fast but still got the job done.

At first it would frustrate me to no end when someone took forever to get to the point or a project moved at a glacial pace. But expecting my team to work faster didn't achieve faster results. It just drove me crazy. Eventually I realized there was only one solution: I had to develop more patience. But how was I supposed to turn myself into a chill person when patience wasn't one of my virtues?

I decided to embark on a personal training program and teach myself to develop patience methodically, the way that Marissa Mayer trained herself to conquer her shyness. I forced myself to slow down, enunciate more clearly and become an active listener. I became conscious of every interaction I had with my staff. I did regular gut-checks to ensure that I wasn't moving too quickly. I constantly asked myself, is this working? Am I being too bossy? Am I pushing beyond an acceptable rate of execution?

If a project wasn't moving at my preferred pace, I investigated the situation to see if it was controllable. Depending on the answers I received, I said, "Let's just minimize further delays, get this out, and do a post-mortem to prevent it from happening again" or "Okay, it is what it is. Let's just deal with the bad news and move on." I also learned to distinguish between the strong per-formers who'd made a calculated decision to push a dead-line for the good of the project ("I wanted to wait for the best director") and the weak ones who'd missed a deadline due to poor time management skills ("I was sidelined working on other projects").

Over time I realized that sometimes projects could only move at a certain pace internally, and that there were often good reasons why one wasn't moving as quickly as I would have liked. Above all, I learned that there's no such thing as a perfect scenario, team member or manager, for that matter. My job was to find the sweet spot between motivating my team and managing my expectations. Retooling a deeply ingrained personality trait didn't happen overnight. It required sustained effort. I rehearsed the techniques daily. But my discipline paid off. Gradually, behaviour that had once been foreign to me became second nature.

Still, while I learned to develop patience, I'm quite sure I'd never even have realized I needed more of it if I'd lacked the capacity for self-awareness. It's so important to nurture that capacity. The higher up you go, the more self-aware you have to become. There's just one catch: the higher up you go, the harder it is to be self-aware. Once you have that fancy title, ego enters the picture. The moment everyone starts looking to you for answers, it's tempting to think you have them all. But I truly believe anyone can develop self-awareness. You just have to make self-reflection a habit. If you're serious about changing, you have to turn the lens on yourself. The more conscious you become, the easier it will be to identify your shortcomings. You might be surprised by what you find.

Some people react emotionally when you ask them a simple question, even though it's obvious to everyone in the room that the question was simply being asked to clarify an issue. They feel as if their credibility is being attacked and react defensively. I coached a woman once who had that problem. After doing some self-examination, she realized her defensiveness had to do with growing up in a family of lawyers. They were always cross-examining her, so even an innocent question felt like an attack to her. Being questioned was one of her triggers.

We all have ghosts in our past. But those ghosts will continue to haunt you in the present if you don't shine a light on them. Once you understand the root of your behaviour, you will rob it of its power over you. Then you're free to work on changing it.

It takes time for defences to form and it takes time to break them down. You won't change right away. But if you know why you're having disproportionately intense reactions, you can begin to pay attention when they're happening. If you sense intense feelings coming on, you'll be in a much better position to control them. The best thing about becoming self-aware though, is that once you understand your behaviour, you'll no longer be at its mercy. And neither will anyone else.

I can't stress enough how critical it is to develop the habit of self-awareness. Unless you're prepared to take a good, hard look at yourself, you'll just keep making the same mistakes, and then you'll never grow as a person or as a leader.

A LOT OF WOMEN are conditioned to believe that ambition is unbecoming. Or they're trained to act as if it's unfeminine and treat it as something that needs masking. They fear if they reveal their ambitions too nakedly they'll be labelled pushy or bossy. These fears are not unfounded. There's plenty of evidence suggesting that women get labelled bitchy or aggressive for behaviour that's seen as laudatory in men, and that some men find powerful women threatening.

On the other hand, many women feel entitled to reach for the stars. Dreaming big isn't their problem. Their problem is thinking that they have to limit their dreams if they want to have a family. Or hesitating to seek promotions even though they're qualified for fear they're not ready or won't be able to manage.

I was taught from an early age that ambition was a good thing to have. I was constantly encouraged to reach beyond my grasp. My mom drilled the message into me from the crib that there weren't any limits to what I could accomplish. I could conquer the world. I heard that refrain so often during my formative years that believing in myself became second nature.

My mother had another mantra: You're in charge of you. She wanted me to have options in life. For that, I had to make my own choices. Control your own future, she'd say. Depend on no one but yourself.

My mom understood ambition. It had emboldened her to leave her marriage. She had no idea what lay in store when she left my dad. She just knew she wanted more for herself and her kids. When I was old enough to understand how powerless she must have felt to lose control over her own future, I made up my mind that I'd always control mine. I never wanted to be in a position where I couldn't buy medicine for my child.

I had another reason to feel comfortable with ambition: growing up in a household with so many brothers. Having all those boys around during my childhood taught me that wanting to win wasn't something to be ashamed of. It was something to be encouraged and lauded. Competition isn't a dirty word to guys. When they play a game, they play to win. They don't downplay their talents or pretend they don't care if they score. They swing for the fences.

Since I lived in my brothers' world, I did whatever they were doing, and usually what they were doing was playing games: baseball, football, hockey, video games, chess, backgammon — you name it. At home, in the back-yard, on family vacations: whatever they did, I did.

I may have been the second oldest (after being knocked from first place when I was eight), but there were six of them and only one of me. If I wanted to get in the game, I had to hold my own. If I wanted to win, I had to out-manoeuvre them. And make no mistake: I wanted to win. Winning was thrilling.

But growing up with boys didn't just teach me how to play the game. It taught me to be tough. When I took a hit, I learned to suck it up. If I fell off my bike, I sucked it up. If a soccer ball hit me in the face, I sucked it up. If an elbow jabbed me in the chin, I sucked it up. Whatever happened, I didn't dare cry. If I cried, they just made fun of me. They told me to stop being such a girl.

To a certain extent I was the right girl for this posse of boys: I enjoy competing, I'm reasonably athletic, and I'm not inclined to wear my feelings on my sleeve. (In university, when my girlfriends and I watched chick flicks, I was the only one with dry eyes.) But growing up in a household of guys definitely upped my game.

In retrospect, I consider myself lucky to have had the upbringing I did. The upheaval of my early childhood toughened me up and made me highly adaptable. Being a child of divorce will do that for you. Above all, it reinforced the message that I should never cede control of my life to others. If I wanted to control my future, I had to take charge. It was an invaluable lesson to learn so young. Between my mom, who taught me to set goals, take risks and keep moving forward, my dad, who taught me the value of hard work, my brothers, who taught me how to play the game and not be a crybaby and my great-grandmother, who taught me to look to the light no matter what life threw in my path, I emerged from my childhood with a ferocious will to succeed.

If you're taught that there aren't any limits, you know what? You can't see any. So when I decided that I wanted to work at FedEx Express Canada, I didn't let the fact that I knew nothing about the transportation industry stop me from applying. Nor did I let the fact the industry was overwhelmingly male-dominated inhibit me. I never allowed such considerations to enter my mind. All I cared about was whether the decision passed my litmus test for making important decisions: Did it make logical sense?

Did it feel right emotionally? Did my gut give me any reason to hold back? The choice felt right on all three counts, so I went for it. (To this day, I rely on my head-heart-gut test to make all major life decisions.)

I WAS LUCKY. I learned to promote my own ambitions early. The data shows, however, that women often hesitate to do so. Either they're socialized to accept what they're offered or their company cultures communicate that message to them. Their reluctance to ask for more is especially noticeable around negotiating for a higher salary.

Research shows that men are more likely to negotiate for the salary they want. In one study, recent male college graduates asked for more money eight times more often than their female counterparts, with the result that the starting salaries of the male MBAs were almost $4,000 higher on average than those of the female MBAs who'd graduated from the same program. Most of the women simply accepted the employer's initial salary offer. In another study, participants were told they'd be paid between $3 and $10 to play a word game. After each game, the researcher said, "Here's $3. Is $3 OK?" In that case, men asked for more money nine times more often than women did. In yet another study, men placed themselves in negotiation situations more often than women did and regarded more of their interactions as potential negotiations. Even in organizations where management makes concerted efforts to treat women fairly and views keeping their employees happy as an important part of their job, women still risk receiving smaller pieces of the pie simply because it doesn't occur to them to ask for more.

I'm one of those women. Even though I have always been extremely proactive about promoting my own career, I never negotiated for a higher salary. I always accepted the one I was offered — even when I became president. I was told that when you jumped from one level to the next from within you received a set increase. Since I'm inclined to follow rules, I accepted the set amount. I assumed that everybody else did as well. It never occurred to me to question it. Looking back, I realize I probably should have asked. A man in my position almost certainly would have. I wish I'd been mentored to negotiate on my own behalf and develop the negotiating skills I needed to do so. Lesson learned.

I came up through the ranks in the '90s and early 2000s, but the problem has by no means gone away. In 2014, after Sony Pictures' emails were famously hacked, it emerged that Jennifer Lawrence and Amy Adams had been offered a smaller percentage of the proceeds from the movie *American Hustle* than male actors Christian Bale and Bradley Cooper. Lawrence later wrote an open letter about the wage gap in which she acknowledged that she found it hard to speak about her experience since her problems weren't exactly relatable. However, she did confess that when she learned how much less she was being paid than her male colleagues, she didn't get mad at Sony. She got mad at herself. She believed she'd failed as a negotiator because she gave up early. She wrote that she didn't want to keep fighting over millions of dollars that, "frankly, due to two franchises, I don't need," but added she'd be lying if she didn't also say that there was an element of wanting to be liked that had influenced her decision to close the deal without a real fight: "I didn't want to seem 'difficult' or 'spoiled.' This could be a young person thing. It could be a personality thing. I'm sure it's both. But . . . based on the statistics, I don't think I'm the only woman with this issue. Are we socially conditioned to behave this way? . . . Could there still be a lingering habit of trying to express our opinions in a certain way that doesn't 'offend' or 'scare' men?"

Clearly there is. Facebook COO Sheryl Sandberg, who's almost twice Jennifer Lawrence's age — and nobody's idea of a shrinking violet — wrote in *Lean In* that when Facebook CEO Mark Zuckerberg made her an offer, she was reluctant to ask for more money until her husband and brother-in-law urged her to negotiate. She said her reluctance stemmed from the fact that Zuckerberg's offer struck her as a fair deal; she was dying for the job and she feared that if she played hardball he might not want to work with her. It was only after her exasperated brother-in-law told her that there wasn't a man at her level who'd accept the first offer that she went back and negotiated hard. As a preamble to negotiations, she told Zuckerberg that since he was hiring her to run his deal teams she'd better show him her chops, and that it would be the only time they'd ever be on opposite sides of the table. She then spent a nervous night wondering if she'd blown it. He came back with an offer extending the length of her contract for another year, which allowed her to buy into the company.

Sandberg later told a reporter that what she found interesting about that story was that when she finally agreed to negotiate because her husband and brother-in-law convinced her no man would ever take the first offer, she felt as if she needed justification. "And it turns out that's what the data says: men can negotiate without apology or justification. It's expected. If women negotiate, they need to justify it. It can't be that you want more for you. Because that's what men get to do."

We know women have the capacity to be great leaders and compete at the highest level. Ability isn't the issue. In a key leadership survey of 7,280 leaders in a range of leadership positions from senior management on down, women outscored men in all but one of the sixteen leadership categories, and in twelve of the sixteen they trounced them. There was only one category in which men outranked women, and it's a telling one: "Develops strategic perspective."

I see this problem time and again when I coach female executives. Ironically, the same women who can strategize brilliantly in a business setting often fail to do likewise when it comes to their own careers. Instead of figuring out a strategy and driving it forward, they keep their heads down, work hard and hope eventually someone will notice and give them a gold star. But passivity doesn't get them promoted. Instead, their bosses keep piling on more work, and they keep quietly seething. Promotions don't drop from the sky any more than counter-offers do. You have to be strategic about getting where you want to go and proactive about asking for what you want. If you don't ask, you don't get. That said, what you receive depends a lot on the way you position your request.

One female executive I mentored had been a director at her company for five years. She wanted to become a VP but her organization didn't have a VP level. The company was structured so that several directors reported directly to the president. She believed that the workload and the challenging assignments that her boss was giving her indicated that he already considered her to be at VP level, but her title and salary weren't commensurate with the role she was playing, and that really ticked her off. She loved the work, but she knew that if she continued to accept the status quo, nothing would change and she'd continue to feel that she was being exploited. What's more, in spite of her performance and results, she knew she'd never get credit for her work. It would always be her boss's show. Something had to change. She was just unsure about how to make a change happen.

I empathized with her frustrations, but I told her that if she wanted to alter the situation, she had to take charge. I advised her to talk to her boss, but warned her not to be confrontational. I said it was really important for her not to make her request about her. If she said, "You're giving me a ton of work and treating me like a VP, so I think I deserve the title and salary to match" — or words to that effect — she'd be dead in the water.

Instead, I suggested she approach the discussion by saying, "I'm happy here. I love what I do and feel really challenged. But I'm interested in advancing in my career and it's unclear where I can go from this point. Where do you see me having the opportunity to move forward?" I explained that if she cast her request in those terms, her boss would be likelier to respond in the way she hoped.

She asked her boss for a meeting and reported back to me that it had gone well. He asked her to think about how she'd envision her role in the company if it had a different structure and requested that she map out what that new structure would look like, and how she pictured her new role evolving within it. She drew up a proposal and gave it to him. Her boss thanked her for the proposal. Then months went by and he didn't get back to her. She became frustrated all over again. "What am I supposed to do now?" she asked me exasperatedly.

I told her that if months had elapsed without any response from her boss, it was entirely reasonable for her to schedule another meeting with him. This time I suggested she ask him out to lunch and say, "Ken, I've given you what I think is a fair amount of time to consider my proposal for structuring the company so that it can be even more successful than it is now. What do you think about my plan? Do you agree with it? Disagree? Do you think it can be implemented? If not, what changes would you recommend?"

I also suggested that she remind him matter-of-factly that she'd been at the same level for five years. To become a COO she had to learn how to do X and Y. If she moved up, she'd be exposed to new challenges, gain new leadership skills and those new skills would provide her with the tools to help her grow the company.

Again, I cautioned her against coming across as whiny, resentful or worse — threatening to quit if he didn't promote her. (Ultimatums are never a smart move unless you're prepared to lose the roll of the dice, which, in my experience, you almost always will.) I also reminded her not to focus on title or salary at that meeting. She had to focus her request on her desire to broaden her role and grow as a businessperson and leader so she could bring new ideas to the company. The time to talk money was *after* her boss agreed to the promotion. At that point it would be clear that if she was going to be assuming more responsibility, she deserved to be paid more money. She followed my advice, and six months later, elatedly emailed me that she'd won the promotion.

I don't think it's ever too early to begin teaching girls that they have to take control of their own futures. I teach my daughters all the time that they can't just sit back passively and wait for their dreams to drop into their laps or someone else to solve their problems. They have to find a way to go after what they want no matter how uncertain, frustrated or discouraged they are. I use the exact same words with them that my mom used with me. *You're in charge of you.* And just as she did with me, I started beating that drum early.

Right now my eldest daughter, Hailey, is in university. Chloe and Mya, my two younger girls, are in high school and Jack is in middle school. I have a few basic non-negotiable parenting rules for all my kids: Don't use drugs. Don't get pregnant or get anyone pregnant. Get good grades. Acquire some form of post-secondary education.

Other than that, I let my kids make their own choices. When it came time for my two older girls to start picking the courses that would steer them towards the path they were going to follow in university, I said I'd help them get started, and guide them along the way, but they had to keep the ball rolling. Like most kids, they want me to solve everything for them. But there's no way I'll do that. Otherwise, how will they learn?

Deciding what career to choose can be a daunting task for a teenager, so when Hailey and Chloe were trying to decide on their courses, I suggested that they think first about the careers they knew for sure that they didn't want to pursue. When I went through the process with Chloe, I asked her if she wanted to become a nurse or doctor. "Oh no, Mom," she said. "I can't stand the sight of blood. "Okay," I said. "Then you probably don't need to take chemistry and biology." That made sense to her. Then I asked if she saw herself as a lawyer. She liked the sound of that. "But you're not taking any law classes, are you?" No, she said, she wasn't.

This prompted me to deliver one of my standard mom lectures. Personally, I don't think you can deliver this lecture often enough, no matter how much eye-rolling it elicits. This is more or less how it goes: Chloe, you're going to set the world on fire. I have no doubt about that. But you need to plan for your future. You need to make thoughtful choices. You can't just sit back and expect someone else to do everything for you. If you're unsure about what to do, go to the school, set up a meeting with your guidance counsellor, ask questions. When life puts a big question mark in your way, don't remain uncertain. Go out and find out what you need to know.

MY FIRST POSITION in the marketing department was essentially nine-to-five, but I usually arrived at work by seven-thirty a.m. to get a jumpstart on my day, and I would stay until six or seven p.m. Pat and I didn't have any kids at this point, so I could stay as late as I wanted. Nobody ever made me work overtime or pressured me to feel that I should. I stayed because I adored my job and was hungry to learn. My job involved working with our company's agency of record under my manager's guidance to produce TV, radio and billboard advertising for our Canadian brand. When it was time to launch a new ad campaign, my manager and I discussed what kind of ad we wanted our agency to create. I wrote the brief. She edited it. We sent it to the agency. They came up with their proposal. We critiqued it. Was it true to the brand? Was it on strategy? Did it have likeability? Then, under her wing, I managed the project through to completion.

I loved my job. One time we flew to Los Angeles to shoot a commercial. The agency had hired an actor to voice the commercial who had been the voice of Mr. Slate, Fred's boss on *The Flintstones*. He pulled up to the studio in a Jag. It was all so exotic and thrilling. I'm sure I had bad days, but I don't remember them. All I remember is loving my boss, loving my job, loving the company and thinking how grateful I was to be able to work at a job I loved every day.

There was craziness, too, of course. I encountered many situations when I had to problem-solve on the fly. One time I was in South Africa to shoot another commercial. We were on set when the director and two agency creative heads began to butt heads. The agency heads were upset that the director was taking their script in a different direction. The three guys got into a territorial fight over creative control. We'd flown halfway around the world to shoot a half-million dollar commercial and the clock was ticking. I faced the very real possibility that the director was going to walk off the set. I had to manage the situation if we were to get the commercial in the can. I jumped into the fray with another woman on the team and the two of us ran interference. We spent the rest of the shoot acting as buffers between the men. It was nuts. But I was learning every day and I soaked up every bit of that knowledge as quickly as I could.

Even though I knew nothing about FedEx before I started researching where to launch my career, my choice has proven to be so right for me that I never left the company. Most people don't stay at the same company for their entire career and people often ask me why I did. I stayed for three reasons: the people, the company culture and because I kept advancing. I often wonder what path my career would have taken if I'd simply tossed my résumé into the wind.

CHAPTER SEVEN

High Hopes

I WAS SO RELIEVED when I learned that Pat had been accepted into Chedoke's program, I think I exhaled for the first time in three months. Not only was its purpose to offer specialized care to patients who had severe, almost irreversible brain trauma, but Dr. Jane Gillett, the medical director, was considered to be a maverick in her field.

I first met Dr. Gillett — or Dr. Jane, as everyone called her — shortly after Pat arrived. She was a tall, earthy woman who wore flowing outfits adorned with colourful stone necklaces and had a calm, almost angelic manner about her. Unlike the other neurologists I'd encountered, Dr. Jane didn't simply view her patients through a narrow medical lens. She considered where her patients would be months and years down the road and how their families were coping with the strain of caring for a loved one in their condition. No matter how busy she was, she always took the time to answer my questions, and she was one of the rare doctors who gave me her personal cellphone number and told me to call whenever I needed her. I didn't just rely on Dr. Jane for medical expertise, though. Often I sought out her counsel about the kids and life in general.

The Chedoke patients had all landed in the unit for different reasons. One man had been severely beaten in in a bar fight. One woman had survived a brain aneurysm. A teenage boy had been seriously injured in a car accident. Pat was the only patient who'd suffered a heart attack. It wasn't until after Pat went to Chedoke that I realized the severity of his brain damage. He was in far worse shape than any of the other patients. All the others had some degree of cognitive ability. None of them could stand, walk on their own or conduct a normal conversation — some were able to say a few words to make their needs known, while others could only grunt and groan — but they all possessed a limited awareness of the world around them. When I walked by the others in the hallway, they were all conscious of someone passing by and they all turned their heads to track my movements. They could also all perform minimal tasks on their own, such as sit upright and eat or blink in response to cue cards. But Pat didn't register a response of any kind. He'd learned to breathe on his own by then, and most of the time he sat slouched over in his wheelchair, his head tilted against the headrest, his eyes open in a vacant stare.

Patients were only supposed to stay in the program for twelve weeks. If they didn't progress during that time, either they'd return home and receive home care or go into a long-term care facility, depending on the family's wishes. If they'd recovered some degree of brain function during the twelve weeks, they'd be transferred to a higher-level cognitive rehab program. That was my hope for Pat. I was especially optimistic about his chances after reading a book that had recently been published about the brain's remarkable capacity for neuroplasticity. Researchers had discovered that with proper stimulation the brain could create new neural pathways around its dormant parts. I was convinced that Pat's brain would start rewiring once the staff began putting him through his paces in rehab. I imagined walking into his room one day and finding him standing beside his bed and saying "Hi." I was sure it was only a matter of time.

For the first week that Pat was at Chedoke I was so ecstatic he'd been admitted to the program when I arrived at the hospital in the morning I practically skipped into the place. On the Monday of his second week in the program, Dr. Jane was waiting for me when I came through the front doors. "I've got this," she said. "He's mine now. It's time for you to return to work. You have to go back and find your new normal."

I KNEW DR. JANE WAS RIGHT to give me my marching orders. Returning to work part-time would be the best thing for me. Still, my boss had told me to take whatever time I needed, and even though I had every confidence Pat was receiving the best care available, had Dr. Jane not given me permission to return to work, I might not have returned so soon. I'd been off work for nearly three months. Without her prodding, I might have taken an indefinite leave of absence and made caring for Pat my full-time job. But she understood something I didn't yet comprehend: when you suffer a loss, you can't let it define you.

Since Pat had taken ill, my life had been consumed with the relentless demands of caring for a sick husband and looking after four small children. Dr. Jane understood that I had to spend at least part of my day in a place where I still had a separate identity; otherwise I wouldn't survive. But even though I knew returning to work was the right decision, I had real anxieties about going back. I was still walking around with a dagger in my heart that I was convinced the whole world could see. How was I going to manage when I felt so vulnerable? It wasn't always predictable when I'd break down. I'd be doing okay, and then something would trigger a memory and I'd come unhinged. What if I lost it in the middle of a meeting? The last thing I needed was a spotlight on me. But I didn't have the luxury of hiding out in my office. Not as a vice-president.

In one sense I was fortunate. In August, when I'd called my boss to give him the news about Pat, he'd asked me what I wanted others to know about my circumstances. I'd requested that he tell the other vice-presidents that

Pat had had a heart attack and the situation wasn't looking good, but that he not give them any other details or send out a mass email.

The rumour mill had started churning right away, of course, but since only a handful of my colleagues knew why I was off work, and none of them knew what was going on, I had the space I needed on re-entry to deal with my feelings without having to deal with their reactions on top. I'll always be grateful to my boss for respecting my privacy and giving me the freedom to confide my news on my own terms when I was ready.

In early November 2007, when I walked through the office doors for the first time since that awful night in August, it was as if I'd crossed the threshold into another world. During the hours I spent beyond those doors, I could escape my life on the other side. Inside, I didn't have to talk about Patrick or care for Patrick or make decisions for Patrick. I just had to focus on my work. Outside, people felt sorry for me. Inside, I was the same person I'd always been.

During my first few months back, work was both a blessing and a curse. On the one hand, it offered me a merciful distraction from my troubles; on the other, it was land-mined with reminders of the life I'd lost. Memories ambushed me at every turn. I'd be in my office trying to concentrate or standing in the cafeteria line waiting to be served, and suddenly I'd be poleaxed by a memory and my mind would start flashing back to the life I'd lost. Once the flashbacks started, I'd have to stand helplessly by and watch fragments of my former life break off and float away into space. It was like enduring an amputation without benefit of anesthetic.

It happened on my first morning back. When Pat was in town, he used to call me around eleven every morning. He didn't like eating the same meal twice in one day, so he always checked in with me before lunch to find out what we were having for dinner that night. It was one of his quirks. I always told him the menu for the week on Sundays when I planned our meals, but by Monday he'd forgotten. When he called we'd chat briefly about dinner, when we planned to be home, and then say goodbye. It was our little ritual. But when the phone didn't ring around eleven that first morning, it hit me hard that he wouldn't be calling.

As the weeks wore on, I also struggled to wrap my head around the event that had shattered our lives. During my drives to and from the hospital, and at other times when my mind was free to wander, my thoughts kept returning to the talk Pat had had with me the night before his heart attack. I couldn't shake the feeling that he'd had some kind of premonition that night. I also continued to wonder if there'd been a reason he'd survived the heart attack. His heart had stopped beating for so long that night the paramedics were shocked when it started up again. I asked the doctors why Pat had survived, but they couldn't give me any answers. In the absence of any rational explanations, I began to look for other reasons why he hadn't been taken from me that night.

At other times, I obsessively parsed the randomness of the tragedy for meaning. Why had he suffered such a cruel fate? What possible reason could there be to cut short the life of a beautiful man and cause such staggering pain to the people who loved him? Why? Why? Why? I was tortured by questions. But the answers never came.

THE TEAM AT CHEDOKE took a holistic approach to treatment. They didn't just provide physiotherapy. They also took their patients' psychological needs into account. For instance, the staff didn't believe in letting patients languish in hospital gowns all day. They considered it therapeutic for patients to wear their own clothing. It was one small way of allowing them to feel human again. At their request, I brought in a few of Pat's wardrobe items and they got him up and dressed every day. The gesture was especially meaningful for me, not only because it afforded him some dignity in circumstances that were anything but dignified, but because Pat had always taken great pride in his appearance. He was such a stylish dresser that people used to call him Mr. GQ.

Dr. Jane had an office at another location, but she came to the hospital a couple of times a week to see patients. Esther was my daily contact concerning Pat's progress, but if I was around when Dr. Jane made her rounds she always sat and talked with me. They both met with me regularly to update me on Pat's care and advise me if there'd been any significant changes in his condition.

I knew from my reading that treating a severe brain injury was a more complicated undertaking than treating an illness like cancer, ALS or MS. Doctors generally knew what to expect from those illnesses and what course of treatment to follow. But brain-injured patients tended to recover differently, even if they'd experienced the same trauma, so the team developed customized treatment programs for each patient.

At the first meeting, Dr. Jane told me that the team planned to conduct a more thorough assessment of Pat and that she intended to try him out on different drugs to see if she could, as she put it, ignite a spark in his brain. She also explained that when a patient had suffered a devastating brain trauma, progress was measured by the tiniest of victories. If the staff could awaken a completely unresponsive patient enough to signal a "yes" or "no" when asked to make a simple choice such as deciding which shirt to wear, that was considered a major milestone. Given Pat's prognosis, she told me their goals had to be small. Mainly they wanted to see if they could get him to respond in some way: perhaps blink or move his finger in response to a question or follow a moving object with his eyes.

SHORTLY AFTER PAT ARRIVED at Chedoke, Dr. Jane enquired whether the kids were asking about his condition and, if so, what I was telling them. I told her they'd been asking whether Daddy was ever coming home, and I said I'd assured them that he would be. It was my practice to tell them that everything was going to be okay. Apart from the fact that I believed those words to be true, I didn't want to frighten them, and my natural instincts as a mother were to give my kids hope and shelter them from pain. But Dr. Jane helped me understand that while it was important to remain hopeful, I'd be doing them a great disservice by giving them false hope, even if I did so with the best of intentions. She said it was critically important for me to be truthful with the children. She pointed out that Hailey and Chloe were old enough to remember this period in their lives. They'd be watching me closely and taking in everything I said. She told me I had to think very carefully about what I told them.

Dr. Jane helped me see that not only was I setting an example through my words and deeds, I was teaching them an invaluable lesson about how to respond to the random unpredictability of life. The reality was that Patrick's prospects were uncertain. If the kids asked whether Daddy was ever coming home, she advised me to qualify my response rather than speak in absolutes. She said a far better way to frame it would be to say "I hope so" rather than "definitely." Her advice was a revelation to me. At the time, I was so consumed with struggling to make it through the day-to-day and find some meaning in the calamity that had befallen our lives, I didn't realize that my choices weren't simply about helping me deal with my own confusion and sadness; they were also about helping my children cope with theirs.

After the kids' first visit with Pat, I brought them to the hospital to see him every Sunday. It was a miracle if they lasted ten minutes. It was basically come, say hi to your dad, okay, let's go to the park. Mya and Jack still had no idea of the direness of his situation; Hailey and Chloe had begun to sense that something was amiss, especially Hailey. The first time the kids visited Pat, his eyes were closed, but after the doctors stabilized his drugs, his eyes opened, and once they did, Hailey didn't understand why he couldn't talk to them. She asked if he was blind. I said I didn't think so. I still don't know how I kept it together when she asked. Generally, though, the kids took their cues from me. If I behaved normally, they were fine.

In November I was not fine. The 20th was Pat's thirty-ninth birthday. I barely made it through the day. Memories stalked me from the moment I opened my eyes that day. I bought a cake. I took the kids to the hospital. We sang "Happy Birthday." It was awful. But the idea of letting the day pass without acknowledgement and pretending that Pat no longer existed was worse.

That month I also received a call from the Mayo Clinic. The kids' blood test results had come back. Hailey and Jack were carriers of Pat's gene. I froze when I heard that news. My mom and I flew down with the kids. The doctor there explained that if a person who carried the gene was lucky enough to have symptoms like a fainting spell, doctors could insert an ICD and put them on a beta blocker. He referred to the gene as "very rare and barely there" and said he didn't think it had caused Pat's heart attack so the kids didn't need to be on beta blockers. But I said that if he couldn't give me 100 percent assurance, then I couldn't live with myself if one of them had a heart attack, so he agreed to prescribe them. He also promised to continue his research and lay the question to rest once and for all.

By December, Pat still hadn't registered a response of

any kind. Nevertheless, I remained hopeful. He'd only been in rehab for a month at that point. The care he was receiving was the gold standard. Dr. Jane seemed to have new drugs to try on him all the time. If the team kept pushing him, and she kept digging into her bag of tricks, anything was possible.

I was especially hopeful because in November my inbox had flooded with emails from friends who'd seen a *60 Minutes* story about severely brain-injured patients who'd awakened from comas years after their doctors had written them off. Anderson Cooper had reported on one man who'd suffered a traumatic brain injury after a car crash. The doctors had told his mother he'd never recover, but she believed he was still in there somewhere, and for years she'd cared for him at home while she continued to search for new treatments. One night she gave him the sleeping pill Ambien when his moaning was keeping her awake; to her astonishment, her son who hadn't spoken a word suddenly became aware and communicative. The show also featured a story about a firefighter who'd been in a coma for ten years. His wife had refused to give up on him as well. Every year on his birthday she brought her four sons to the nursing home. One day she received a call from the home to say he'd awakened and was asking for his family.

The patients who'd experienced these awakenings were considered to be in a minimally conscious state. I was well aware that there was a significant difference between their conditions and Pat's. Minimally conscious patients possess some degree of cognitive awareness and tend to improve, albeit in a limited way, whereas patients in a vegetative state lack any cognitive function, and their conditions generally persist. Nevertheless, I continued to hope. Besides my kids, hope is what got me out of bed in the morning, hope is what allowed me to put one foot in front of the other and hope is what gave me the strength to carry on. I wasn't about to surrender it without a fight.

Once November turned into December, I began thinking about Christmas. Pat and I had a Christmas tradition: I did all the shopping for the kids and put them to bed on Christmas Eve. He stayed up until two or three in the morning wrapping gifts. Christmas morning, when I came downstairs with the kids to the sight of all the presents sparkling under the tree, the moment was just as magical for me as it was for them. When it hit me that Pat wouldn't be around to wrap the gifts that year, I became paralyzed with dread. How on earth would I make it through Christmas?

We have an expression around the office that our culture consultant taught us: don't get mad at gravity. It means you should focus your energies on what you can control and let go of the things you can't. I still had high hopes that Pat would recover but no control over how quickly he'd improve. My dread of the holidays was suffocating. But there wasn't any point in dreading gravity. I had to focus on what I could control. If I allowed myself to think ahead, if I opened that door even a crack, my anticipatory anxiety would consume whatever limited emotional reserves I possessed. And those I could not afford to squander. So I didn't allow myself to think ahead. I told myself Christmas was still a few weeks away. There wasn't any point in worrying about it now. I'd seen how quickly life could change. If it could change that quickly for the worse, then why couldn't it change that quickly for the better? It was still early days. This Christmas, I'd figure it out. Next Christmas, my VP of Wrapping would be back.

IN KEEPING WITH CHEDOKE'S PHILOSOPHY of integrating patients with their families as much as possible, the staff had been encouraging me to bring Patrick home for a couple of weeks over Christmas. Early in December, I'd begun making the arrangements. Bringing Pat home was a massive undertaking. I had to organize twenty-four-hour care, and order a hospital bed, wheelchair ramps and a special machine to transfer him from wheelchair to bed. A couple of weeks before Christmas, I was in the process of arranging movers to clear the furniture out of our living room to accommodate the hospital bed when I was pulled out of a meeting at work to take an emergency call. It was the hospital. Pat had developed a serious case of pneumonia and had been transferred to Hamilton General. I was to get there immediately.

I was crying so hard on my way to the hospital I could barely see the road. *Don't you dare die, Patrick Lisson. Don't you dare die. I'm not ready to let you go.* I threw the car into park, raced inside, pushed through the ER doors and frantically scanned the room. As I stood frozen in place searching for him, I felt a hand on my arm. It was a nurse. "He's in bed number eleven," she said. "He's very sick. He has a high fever. But he's not going to die." The moment I heard those words, I calmed down.

Pat didn't make it home that Christmas. Christmas Day he had a high fever. The kids and I spent Christmas morning at the house and the afternoon at the hospital. They didn't want to go. They didn't understand why they had to. Daddy was supposed to come home for Christmas. They wished him a half-hearted Merry Christmas and asked if they could go home and play with their toys.

I broke down in front of them that day for the first time. Mya and Jack just stared. They had no idea what was happening. Hailey and Chloe tried to console me. "It's okay, Mom," Hailey said. "Everything's going to be okay." But I could see by the way she looked at me that she knew everything was not going to be okay. Everything was terribly, terribly wrong.

CHAPTER EIGHT

Managing Expectations

YEARS EARLIER, long before I had to manage Pat's care and wrangle hospital teams and cope with the countless complexities of the medical system, I had to navigate a different kind of uncharted territory — the kind I encountered when I first took on managerial responsibilities at FedEx.

In June 1996, when I was appointed marketing manager, I'd been in the department long enough to know how things worked, but suddenly I had to manage a team, assume responsibility for the careers of five people, oversee our entire advertising and communications strategy and become answerable for all of our radio, print and outdoor ad campaigns, promotions, direct mail programs and local event marketing. I was twenty-seven years old.

I realized the biggest misstep I could make was to start throwing my weight around. I'd seen how some people behaved once they'd gained a bit of power and I made a point to never behave like that. I certainly never wanted to work for a boss who dictated rather than listened, and I knew how my colleagues viewed bosses who were legends in their own minds. I wasn't going to win anyone over by giving a lecture. Instead, I began by asking questions.

My first week on the job I met individually with my team and asked for their thoughts on what was working well and what needed improvement. They talked. I listened, asked questions and took notes. A week later I called the team together, thanked them for their input, said we couldn't fix everything and suggested we tackle the fixable items starting with the first three on my list. Then I solicited their input. I took that approach every time I was promoted.

EARLIER, I SAID that when I was at a junior level I asked my mentors how to advance, and they told me to make a lateral move whenever I had the chance. They explained that if I seized those opportunities when they arose, I'd broaden my experience, increase my value to the company and position myself for a promotion. The first chance I had to develop a new area of expertise arose a year or so into my stint as marketing manager when the product development manager left the company. I could easily have stayed where I was, but I had bigger plans, so in the fall of 1998 I leapt at the chance to make a move.

As manager of products and pricing, I had to oversee our annual pricing strategy, manage our drop boxes, and learn how to launch new products. The position required me to become far more analytical than I'd had to be as a manager of marketing and communications. While direct mail involves analytics to some degree, decisions around marketing and promotion are much more subjective in nature. I have an analytical mind, but I'm really more of a right-brain person. However, you need both sides of your brain in the business world.

Not only did I have to develop a grasp of statistics and economics, but for the first time, I had to come up with a hardcore business case to launch new products, and back up my judgment calls with data. I'd prepared business cases in school, but those were all theoretical. Now if I made an error in judgment, it could have serious financial implications.

This was new territory and I certainly would not have been inclined to venture into it on my own. But taking that leap forced me to conquer my fears. In the process, I developed the data-and-number-crunching hemisphere of my brain and learned to speak an entirely new business language. Most importantly, mastering the unknown bolstered my confidence.

WE KNOW THAT WOMEN are brimming with talent, ambition and leadership ability. We know that teams with more women on them have a greater collective intelligence, and that boards with women outperform their rivals, deliver higher returns on equity and are more aggressive about taking initiative and refusing to accept poor company performance. Indeed, there's such an avalanche of evidence that companies earn a higher yield on their investment when they promote women to leadership positions, you'd think C-Suites and boardrooms would be brimming with them.

And yet, although women make up forty-seven percent of the workplace in Canada, they comprise only three percent of CEO positions. Less than a quarter of senior managers in the country are women, and women don't gain equal access to resources, venture capital and other forms of investment, either. When the *Globe and Mail* surveyed Canadian corporations in 2015, the majority of executives polled had no women on their boards. Not one.

Given the benefits that accrue to companies that promote women to leadership positions, you'd think savvy executives would be standing on street corners with sandwich boards begging the best and brightest female leaders to join their ranks. But one-third of the executives polled in that *Globe and Mail* survey said the stats didn't bother them.

"Not enough qualified candidates" is the reason usually floated for the lack of women at the highest echelons. But given the amount of female firepower in this country, blaming women for their lack of representation at that level ignores very real systemic issues that prevent them from advancing at a rate commensurate with their talents and abilities: gender discrimination, a lopsided division of labour on the home front and still unequal pay structures. The fact that entrenched social, institutional and attitudinal barriers prevent women from advancing to the top isn't even arguable anymore.

But no matter how often I read the data on all the systemic barriers preventing women from making it past the glass ceiling, I can't help feeling that one of the strongest barriers women face is one within: their tendency to indulge their self-doubt more often than men do because of the way they've been socialized.

Despite being just as qualified as men, research suggests that women often hold themselves back because they don't consider themselves as ready for promotions as men, predict they'll do worse on tests, underestimate their abilities or attribute them to luck. I know so many women who fit that description. But if you can't even acknowledge your own power, how can you possibly expect others to acknowledge it?

When women talk to me about why they don't plan to seek a promotion or pursue a career dream, I often hear statements like these: "There isn't enough time in the day as it is." "There's no way I can go for a promotion. I'm not qualified." "I don't have enough experience to strike out on my own in this economy." "I want to have a baby, so I'll stay in a job I know I can do." "Female CEOs are a breed apart. They're the exception. I could never achieve their level of success."

If you have ambitions to move up but are telling yourself that story, I'm convinced you'll never get ahead. All the great mentors I've had, male or female, have had one thing in common: *they believed in their own success.* So, as much as I think that we have to address all the external barriers holding women back, I believe women have a responsibility to ask themselves whether they have any internal barriers holding them back as well. One barrier I see a lot of women struggling to surmount is their desire for perfection.

I've met many women who think they have to be 100 percent qualified before they put themselves forward for a promotion. But in my opinion that's a mistake. You can't put your career on hold just because everything's not perfect. If you always insist on perfection, you'll never accomplish anything. Besides, nobody's ever 100 percent qualified for a promotion. I interviewed for the president's job a few years before I was appointed. I knew that winning the job then was a long shot. Nevertheless, I applied. And even though I was told I wasn't ready, I've never regretted applying. I gained valuable experience interviewing for a top-level position and put myself on the radar for next time.

If you're hesitant to put your toe in the water until it's the perfect temperature, consider this: men don't demand perfection of themselves before they put themselves out there. The data shows that they have conversations about advancing earlier in their careers, more frequently and with more assertiveness than women. Of course, men have a head start in learning to be assertive — they're encouraged to be that way from the crib. There's no question that the issue is more complicated for women because of the way they're socialized. But just because an issue is more complicated doesn't mean it's insurmountable. If you're serious about advancing, then ask yourself whether you're waiting for the perfect scenario before you make a move. If you are, then you're limiting yourself.

Thankfully I learned early in my career not to wait for the perfect circumstances before leaping. Pat and I were planning to start our family around the time I was promoted to marketing manager. Since I'd just taken on a much more demanding job, I was uncertain about whether it was the right time to add a kid to the mix. I asked one of my female mentors for advice and she gave me wise counsel. She said if Pat and I were ready to start our family, then we should go for it. If I waited for everything to be perfect, we'd never start. After all, when was life ever perfect?

So here's my advice: Don't wait for spring. Do it now. If you have doubts, which you no doubt will, make a conscious effort to dial them down.

EVERY WOMAN HAS TO DEAL with the double standard at some point in her career. I first became conscious of it after I started having kids. After Hailey was born, I can still recall the anxiety I felt the first time I had to excuse myself from a meeting in order to make daycare pickup. With Pat travelling so much, unless my parents picked up the kids, I was on call most nights for the first four years. Pickup time was six p.m. To make it on time, I had to be out the door by five on the dot. If I had a meeting that ran past five, I had no choice but to excuse myself. If

I was chairing a meeting, I ended it and said we'd follow up on unfinished business another time or I asked a team member to take over, keep me posted and said I'd conference in later if I could. If someone else was chairing the meeting, I said I'd check back afterwards to learn what I'd missed and make up the work later that evening.

Nobody ever said a word to me about leaving those meetings early, but every time I had to stand up and excuse myself I had a knot in my stomach. Pretty soon I started dreading late afternoon meetings. If I had one scheduled for four p.m., I worked myself up into a state of high anxiety worrying that it would run late. In fact, worrying about whether a four o'clock meeting would run over caused me far more anxiety than presenting to senior management. And I was always apologizing to someone: to my team for having to wrap up before the meeting was over; to the other chairs for having to excuse myself; to the daycare sitter for arriving late for pickup; to my kids for making them wait.

No doubt some of the pressure I felt was self-imposed, but it was impossible not to worry I'd be perceived as less committed than my male colleagues or fear that by leaving early I'd miss out on important information and be cut out of the loop. I felt resentment, too. After all, many of the family men in the room had the same career ambitions as I had. Why was I the only one that had to leave while they all got to stay?

For the first two years, I felt so alone. After Chloe was born, another woman with a six p.m. daycare pickup joined our team. The first time she stood up at five o'clock and said she had to leave I almost high-fived her. Still, while I felt much less alone after she came aboard, her arrival didn't change the fact that men and women weren't playing on a level playing field. There was a double standard, and it was a problem. And it wasn't going away any time soon.

I knew that if I wanted to be taken seriously I had to be heard. But I also knew that if my male colleagues perceived me to be emotional, they'd tune me out. The first order of business, then, was getting them to listen to me. I decided that no matter how upset I was I would never reveal my feelings. If I advocated for a decision and it didn't go my way, I wouldn't let on how I was feeling and I wouldn't carry my feelings out of the boardroom. I'd be the unflappable one.

I want to make it clear that I'm not saying you can't bring your emotions to the workplace. It's human to express emotions, and doing our jobs would be extremely boring if we couldn't bring passion to the task. But you have to keep your emotions in check. Whether you're male or female, you have to maintain your composure in a tense situation. If somebody asks you a tough question, you can't go all red in the face or sit there with tears running down your face. And you can't pound your fist on the table just because you don't like the way the wind's blowing. I'm not keen to witness a temper tantrum whether the person throwing it is a man, a woman or one of my kids. Nor is anyone else. You have to find other outlets for your aggression.

To keep mine in check, I trained like a soldier. I studied

techniques to control my emotions. I taught myself to develop a poker face. When I was angry, I sat on my hands and counted to ten so I wouldn't lose control. If I hit a wall with a difficult person, I breathed deeply, thought ahead a couple of steps, and tried to come up with a solution to offer them to overcome the barrier in their mind.

If emotions were running high in the room but I thought the meeting was salvageable, I said let's take five. A break gave everybody the chance to cool off, gather their wits and return with a renewed sense of purpose. If I was dealing with a completely irrational person, I said we weren't going to resolve the matter today and suggested reconvening after we'd had a chance to step back and rethink the issue. Learning to keep calm and carry on took time, discipline and focus.

I also learned to manage my response to bad news. Some bosses blow up when they receive bad news. But if you lose your temper, your staff will be afraid to come to you and the problem will only get worse. The more leadership experience you gain, the more you realize that bad news is rarely catastrophic. Things tend to work themselves out. But when I first became a manager, every bit of bad news felt like the end of the world.

When I was still relatively new to the job, one of the senior people in charge of our advertising came into my office and told me we weren't going to hit the airdate for our commercials. When you plan to run commercials around key times of the year to attract the biggest audience and invest millions to target that audience, not hitting your airdate is a big deal. When I heard that news I flipped out. "What? What do you mean? How could this happen?"

I spent most of that night worrying about having to tell my boss the news the next day. But when I delivered it, the first words out of her mouth were, "Alright, are you sure there's nothing we can do?" As soon as she asked that question I realized I'd never even asked it.

Her response taught me how poorly I'd handled the situation. Freaking out about the situation was a mistake. I should have focused on what it would take to remedy it.

After that, I trained myself to stay calm whenever I received bad news. I ask the why questions later, but in the moment the first thing I say is always, "Okay, is there anything we can do to fix the problem?"

NEXT, I WENT TO WORK on my communication style. I'd observed that if women took forever to make a point or raised their voices in an effort to be heard, men's eyes glazed over. So I thought carefully before I spoke, spoke only when I had something to say, kept my message crisp and my delivery low-key.

Once when I was presenting, this one individual kept raising points that were completely irrelevant to the outcome. I could see that he was succeeding in hijacking my presentation with his constant interruptions, and I could feel my blood starting to boil. But under pressure my training kicked in. I took a few deep breaths, bit my tongue and suggested that he and I have a separate meeting to address his concerns so that I could complete my presentation in the allotted time. However, since I'm not a robot, I had to find ways to release my feelings; otherwise the stress would have eaten me alive. Some people find the gym to be a great outlet. I preferred to go home and vent to Patrick.

I also learned not to let anyone cut me off when I was speaking. You can't shrink from those situations. If you allow yourself to be silenced, you'll lose all credibility. But you have to assert yourself without being confrontational. You have to take back control in a diplomatic way. Another time a colleague kept interrupting me, I said, "Oh, excuse me. May I just finish my thought, please? I have about five more points to make, and then you can have the floor." He didn't open his mouth again. How you deliver your message is key. Your delivery determines how the other person will react. If it's respectful, you'll be heard. If it's sarcastic, the person will attack.

Since workplace rules were historically written by men, some women feel the only way they'll be taken seriously is by behaving in the way they think a man would behave in the same circumstances, and walk in the room with guns blazing. But a woman who does that is more likely than a man to be judged for the behaviour. So while I understand why some women might feel compelled to adopt that stance, those who do, in my observation, invariably shoot themselves in the foot.

It was never my style to attack another person. At the same time, I was wary of coming across as too nice. When women are too nice, men often interpret their niceness as a signal that they can't make the tough calls. I wanted

Patrick and I throughout the years — from high school to our wedding day, January 22, 1994.

Patrick and our
girls, Hailey,
Chloe, and Mya.

(top) Patrick and
Jack in May 2007.

Hailey, Chloe, Mya
and Jack in May
2007 at my cousin
Libby's wedding
in Mexico. Patrick
had his heart attack
three months later.

(left) The last picture I have of
Patrick: this was taken the weekend
of his heart attack.

(top) One of my favourite pictures as
this captures the true essence of my
Patrick and his beautiful smile.

Mya's sixth birthday, two months after Patrick's heart attack.

My mom, stepdad and me at my birthday dinner in 2017.
I don't know what I would do without them.

My mom, stepdad, Jack and me at Jack's school when he won an award in 2016.
They come to every special moment in my children's lives. I'm very blessed.

My mom, Hailey, Chloe, Mya and me at one of our girls lunches in 2016.
Three generations of LOVE.

© André Van Vugt

Looking forward, not looking back as I'm not going that way.

to achieve a balance between those two extremes, and a delivery style that felt authentic to me.

Finding the right balance took time. But I tinkered with my delivery and eventually I found a way to offer constructive criticism in a firm but compassionate way. I spoke clearly and began with the positives. Only after I'd covered the areas where I believed the person had done well did I suggest ones where I thought there was room for improvement. I still made my points without pulling my punches, but I found that if I leavened my criticism with empathy, the person didn't have to walk away from the exchange feeling as if they'd had the wind knocked out of them. Again, finding my footing came down to patience and practice. But eventually I found a way to project confidence in a powerful way.

No woman gets a free pass when it comes to the double standard. The key to dealing with it, I believe, is refusing to let it distract you. Prime Minister Justin Trudeau appointed Katie Telford to be his chief of staff when she was thirty-seven. Telford's colleagues have said that throughout her career she has had to deal with misperceptions based on her age, gender and physical stature, and she has often surprised seasoned political operatives with her ability to make tough calls and hold others to account.

Another powerful woman who has spent her career dodging the double standard and found an ingenious way around it is professional poker player Annie Duke. Duke won a $2 million jackpot in the Tournament of Champions and a gold bracelet at the World Series of Poker in 2004

— she was the only woman in competition. To get to the final hand she'd knocked out ten of the best players in the world. Nevertheless, she later told a reporter that she felt she didn't deserve to be sitting at that table.

Duke said she believed the only reason she'd been invited to participate in the game was because the organizers needed a token woman and her presence was considered to be good optics. Throughout the game, a message ran constantly as background noise in her brain: You don't deserve a seat at the table. You just got lucky. Duke was certain that sooner or later everyone would discover she was an imposter. She felt this way despite the fact that she'd made her living playing poker at the highest level of the game for the previous ten years.

Psychologists call this phenomenon "stereotype threat." The theory goes that if you think people have a certain stereotype about you because of your gender, race, age or sexuality, a part of you is afraid that your actions will prove that stereotype true. Since you're worried, you get distracted. And then the stereotype actually has a good chance of coming true.

But Duke figured out a way to not only conquer that doubting inner voice, but to use the double standard to her advantage. She reasoned that if her opponents were so deeply emotionally invested in the idea that she was a woman, then probably they weren't going to make good decisions against her at the poker table. Instead of allowing herself to become rattled by their stereotypical assumptions, she devised a strategy to make them pay for having them.

She mentally divided the men who held sexist stereotypes about her into three categories: the flirting chauvinists, the disrespecting chauvinists and the angry chauvinists. She used flirting to her advantage with the flirting chauvinists, but only at the table. She never went on a date with any of them. The disrespecting chauvinists she bluffed. Bluffing worked with them because she confounded their expectations. They didn't expect her to bluff because they assumed women lacked creativity and avoided taking risks. She couldn't bluff the angry chauvinists because they so feared being beaten by a woman they'd do anything to avoid that fate. But their fear made them reckless, so she used patience as a weapon and bided her time until she saw an opportunity to trip them up.

Duke didn't get mad. She got even. Instead of leaving the table in a huff, she controlled her emotions, told herself she'd deal with them later and had a good cry on the way home. But by the time she'd made it to the final table, she'd so refined her techniques for outwitting her unwitting sexist opponents, she was invincible.

I love stories about defying the odds — especially stories with female heroines. I identify with those stories. What I love about them most is how everyone is always telling the heroine how she'll never accomplish her goal but the heroine refuses to listen — even when her inner voice is telling her that maybe they're right.

If somebody tells me something can't be done, it just spurs me to try harder. I find naysayers motivating that way. It's not that I don't have doubts. I have doubts all the time. It's just that I refuse to lend them any credence.

Belief is the engine behind every successful endeavour. If you want to succeed, you have to believe that you can. And you have to continue believing in yourself no matter how daunting the obstacles. I truly believe that the conversation you have with yourself is the pivotal factor in whether you'll succeed. I believe I'll succeed. Looking back, I think it's one of the main reasons I did.

AS I MOVED UP through the ranks at FedEx, one of my mentors told me that since some deals closed on the golf course, it would probably be a good idea for me to learn how to play the game. I know female executives who would not take kindly to such advice. Again, while I empathize with that point of view, I don't subscribe to it. If the golf course was where the action was, then I wanted to be in on it. I learned to play.

Initially, I viewed learning to play golf as part of my job, but I actually wound up liking the game. I enjoyed its competitive aspects and I grew to appreciate its mental challenges as well. On the plus side, our house backed onto a golf course, so I didn't have far to go to practise. And since Pat was a golfer, I loved that it was something we could do together. I asked him to take me out a few times to hit balls. I also hired an instructor, so I wouldn't look like a complete idiot on the course. Sometimes I did look like a complete idiot, of course. Golf can be a humbling experience, as any seasoned golfer will tell you. But I refused to worry about what others thought. I just went out there and took my best shot.

Learning to golf allowed me to get to know my customers outside of the work environment. Connecting with them in a relaxed setting gave me insight into their business challenges and provided me with valuable information that helped me negotiate more effectively when it was time to renew their contracts.

Networking is everything in business. Sometimes I get to know our customers on the golf course. Sometimes I invite business associates to fundraising events. You can't buy the goodwill that flows from those gestures, so I work very hard at nurturing my connections. In 2015, when I was being inducted into WXN's Top 100 Hall of Fame, I invited two female executives I was mentoring to sit at my table. They were so thrilled for the opportunity to network in that crowd you'd think I'd sent them to Paris for the weekend.

All my mentors stressed how important it was for me to participate in work social functions, too, so I tried to never miss those, either. I remember hearing people say they weren't going to the company Christmas party. I happen to like going to parties, so I always looked forward to attending ours. But even if attending the company Christmas party were my least favourite thing to do and I'd had to fly in to attend from Antarctica, I wouldn't have missed it. You have to show up if you want to succeed. Showing up demonstrates commitment. Some people have other priorities. They think, why bother? I think that attitude could be severely career limiting.

The workplace is a very different place today than it was when I came up. Twenty-five years ago, I felt I had to adapt to male ideas about how leaders were supposed to act to be taken seriously. Today, I have adopted a leadership style that's authentic to me. And that's as it should be. You shouldn't have to turn yourself into a pretzel to accommodate somebody else's ideas about the correct way to lead. Allowing for diverse viewpoints is better for everyone. And, as the data shows, it's also better for the bottom line. That's why I believe diversity is the future. And the day will come when nobody will know what you mean when you talk about the double standard.

AFTER I BECAME a senior marketing specialist, I was assigned to come up with recommendations for where to locate our new drop boxes. I decided to drive around and look at the drop boxes we already had in place. Some were due for a new paint job. I also pulled a report and discovered some weren't doing any volume, even though we were sending a courier out to them every day.

When I presented my report, I didn't just recommend locations for our new drop boxes. I suggested refurbishing the ones that needed repair and moving the poorly performing ones to higher volume locations. I framed my report by saying I'd uncovered additional information during my research and included recommendations based on the information I'd found. By going that extra mile, I showed my superiors I was already performing at the next level and conditioned them to see me as an obvious choice for promotion when an opportunity arose.

I didn't just go beyond what was expected of me when

I was given a task, though. I told my bosses I'd do extra work and volunteered for special assignments. When those assignments arose, I was tapped to chair them. As marketing manager, I was asked to chair a special task force on improving our cross-border business and report on our progress to senior managers. Projects like that put me on the radar of senior management.

I was promoted to director of marketing in December 1999, a few months after Chloe was born. Two years later, when I was seven months pregnant with Mya, I was given the opportunity to lead a team charged with developing a worldwide customer experience strategy for our company. At the time, every region developed its own strategy. I had to assemble teams of managers and directors from around the world and lead a two-day meeting at head office in Memphis where we had to come up with a presentation to make recommendations to the FedEx senior leadership team in Memphis.

The night before the meeting, our team went out for dinner to a barbecue joint. Everybody ordered pulled pork. I ordered chicken. The next day, everybody else was fine and I came down with a nasty case of food poisoning. I felt the first rumblings shortly before show time. But the show had to go on. I spent the day mainlining Gatorade and excusing myself whenever I had to make a dash for the ladies' room. To this day, I have no idea how I made it through that meeting.

If you're looking for a learning experience, I don't recommend chairing your first worldwide strategy meeting battling a severe case of food poisoning while ripe with child. You can find better learning opportunities. But it was my leadership of this particular strategy meeting that once again put me on my bosses' radar.

In that moment, however, probably the biggest lesson I learned was that no matter how thoroughly I planned and organized, there'd always be curveballs I didn't see coming. I had to expect them, and deal with the consequences in the best way I could; otherwise, they would knock me sideways.

CHAPTER NINE

Why Isn't This Working?

EARLY IN MY CAREER my mentors told me to start writing down my goals, so I began making that a regular practice. It's one of the best ways I've ever found to help me visualize a goal I want to achieve. To this day I record my short and long-term personal and professional goals on lists and review them a few times a month. Reviewing them keeps them fresh in my mind and helps me reflect on the baby steps I have to take to achieve them. I jot down those steps along with the deadline I have in mind. That simple routine keeps me focused and prevents me from becoming so consumed by the present moment that I forget to keep my eye on the future.

It doesn't matter how small or large my goal is. It can be something as mundane as losing weight or as monumental as writing a book. All I know is that if you commit to recording your goals and are consistent about following through on taking the steps required to make them happen, you'll have a much better chance of getting where you want to go.

Case in point: during each pregnancy I gained fifty pounds, and after every one, between ten to twenty of those pounds hung around afterwards. So each time I gave birth I wrote, "Get back in shape" on my list. Some people enjoy exercise. I am not one of those people. I do, however, enjoy achieving goals. So I visualized myself wearing my favourite jeans again, found a fitness buddy (which was key for me) and committed to doing a physical activity three times a week. I didn't hire a trainer. I didn't sign up for CrossFit. I just went for power walks. I was disciplined about my routine, though: I went three times a week, rain or shine. I stuck to my plan and lost the weight every time.

When I was marketing manager, I wrote "Become president" on my goal list. I didn't see any reason why I couldn't become the president of the company so I didn't allow myself to think that becoming the president was too daunting a goal. I just focused on doing whatever I could to move in that general direction. I didn't worry about the path. I focused on the destination.

After I became president, I started doing a lot of speaking. At speaking engagements, people often asked me if I had a book. When I said I didn't, they encouraged me to write one. I wrote "Write a book" on my goal list. That goal sat on my list for more than two years. During that time I continued to give speeches and people continued to ask me if I had a book. It took me more than two years to wrap my head around the possibility that I had a story people would want to read. And then one Sunday afternoon I was sitting at home, and I looked at my list and wondered what step I could take that day to move towards accomplishing that goal. I knew that if I did decide to write a book, I would need a writer's help, so I reached out to some of my connections and they put me in touch with some people in publishing. The conversations I had with those people helped me figure out whether to proceed, and, if so, what my next steps should be.

The point is that if I hadn't written down my goal you wouldn't be reading this book today. That's where it all started. I wrote down my goal. Then I put my desire to write a book out into the universe. Talking to others opened doors. One thing led to another and here I am.

When I tell people that writing down my goals helped me succeed, it sounds far too easy to them. They think I have some deep dark secret and I'm holding out on them. But the act of making tangible something that is intangible is an incredibly powerful tool.

You can't just write down your goals and forget about them. You have to make inching towards them a regular part of your life. Ask yourself what's the one thing you can do tomorrow that you didn't do today that will take you closer to your goal. You need the discipline it takes to stick with an exercise routine. But, as with exercise, many people give up. Or they begin with good intentions and lose interest. Then their goals wind up languishing in a drawer somewhere. Visualization may be powerful, but without commitment it's no match for inertia.

And yet, as much as I believed in visualization and had reaped its rewards, after Pat had his heart attack I was forced to accept that it had its limitations. I had to face that no matter how diligently I set goals for myself and determinedly worked towards achieving them, some goals were simply beyond my reach.

PAT SPENT THREE WEEKS at Hamilton General after Christmas, recovering from pneumonia. By mid-January he'd still failed to achieve any of the standard markers and he was still in worse shape than any of the other patients. The deadline for his stay at Chedoke was fast approaching. With each passing day I grew more and more desperate for a signal that he was responding to treatment: a blink, a twitch of the finger, *something*.

In late January, Dr. Jane called a meeting. "Lisa," she said, "you know we're coming up to the three-month mark. You know we only keep patients here for that long because if we're going to see an impact from what we do here, we're usually going to see it within that time frame. Given that Pat hasn't shown any improvement, I think we have to be realistic about his chances. But we've decided to keep him on for another couple of months. We want to see if there's anything else we can do to ignite a spark."

I felt as if I'd won the lottery. A two-month reprieve

may not sound like a long time, but it meant that for two more months I didn't have to worry about Pat's care. For two more months I could continue to hope for a miracle.

Up until that point, I'd always defined a miracle as total recovery. After that meeting however, my expectations began to shift. For the first time I began considering the possibility that maybe Pat's comeback might be less dramatic than I'd hoped. For the first time I began to entertain the notion that maybe he wouldn't recover 100 percent. I started telling myself, okay, maybe he won't walk again, maybe his speech will be slurred. If that happens, it won't be the end of the world. As long as he can communicate, I'll be fine.

It broke my heart to think of him awakening to the news that he'd have to spend the rest of his life in a wheelchair. But I consoled myself with the knowledge that Pat was basically an optimistic person. He'd need time to come to terms with his situation, but with our love and support, eventually he'd adjust. Eventually he'd realize he was lucky to be alive. Still, just in case there was an experimental drug Dr. Jane didn't know about, I began reading the medical journals again. Maybe I could find a miracle drug she hadn't tried.

ONCE UPON A TIME — before I had kids — I thought that all it took to ensure life would unfold in an orderly fashion was to plan ahead. All I needed to guarantee it would run smoothly were foresight and organizational skills, and I had both in spades. So after Hailey was born, I bought one of those big desk calendars to manage our lives. Pat and I entered all our dates on it: work obligations, travel schedules, his nights out with the boys, mine with the girls.

That calendar was our lifeline. Months before we were scheduled to move into our new house, I blacked out moving week on the calendar and designated it a no-fly period. However, no matter how carefully I planned, inevitably there were screw-ups. Sometimes I found out at the last minute that Pat would be away. At such times, the conversation went something like this: "Why didn't you tell me you were going to be away?" "I did tell you." "Why didn't you write it down?" "I forgot."

I'd panic. Then I'd go into crisis intervention mode. I'd say, "Okay, I can cover Monday and Wednesday, but what about Tuesday and Thursday? I'll see if my mom's available." (I might have said a few other things, too.) When we both had to travel at the same time, the stress was off the charts. It was a flawed system to be sure: unpredictable, reactive and far from fail-safe. But for the first two kids, we muddled through. I learned to take those moments in stride, stay solution-focused, and, above all, not to expect perfection.

Having kids — not to mention an inconvenient bout of food poisoning — had taught me that life didn't always go according to plan. Before Pat had his heart attack, I'd had anxious moments when things went awry. But after I'd problem-solved, they'd always sorted themselves out. After his heart attack, I tried to convince myself that the same rules applied. I reasoned it was only a matter of time before Pat would be back to normal and we'd carry on with our beautifully chaotic lives. I was starting to realize, however, that not everything in life could be sorted out — no matter how hard you tried.

After I'd been back at work for a few months, and the pain that had blindsided me daily began to subside to a dull ache, I had to confront the fact that my life would never be the same. I'd made the decision to keep Pat on life-support. It was the path I'd chosen. Now I had to follow it through to the end. Travelling from home to work to hospital and repeating the cycle with no end in sight was my reality now. The only way I'd survive was by finding ways to live beyond my sadness.

Besides Jojo and my parents, about the only thing I could count on with any certainty during that time was my routine, and I drew comfort from its structure and predictability. I arrived at the office around eight a.m., stayed until around two in the afternoon, then made the hour or so commute to see Patrick. I generally made it home by seven so I could spend some time with the kids before bedtime. My travel schedule didn't resume right away; otherwise my work responsibilities remained the same. I managed my workload by delegating a lot more than I had before. After the first few months, work became my therapy. At work, when problems arose, I knew how to fix them. The rules still applied.

I didn't share my news with all of my colleagues until I was back for four or five months. I wasn't ready to open up until then, or bring my sorrow into my sanctuary. When I did finally confide in a few individuals, they said, "*What? This is what you've been dealing with? I had no idea.*"

I'd never doubted that my colleagues would be supportive when they heard my news, but I feared they'd pity me, and that I could not bear. To my surprise, their reactions gave me strength. Instead of making me feel diminished, they made me feel that I was conducting myself with grace, and that knowledge helped me carry on.

The first few months Pat was at Chedoke, I was convinced he'd recover, so I didn't worry about the future. But as time began to close in on me, I became increasingly preoccupied with his fate. If he didn't improve, I had no idea where Dr. Jane was going to send him. And if I didn't know, I couldn't plan. Not knowing was killing me. I'd be in a meeting and my mind would start wandering and someone would ask me a question and it would snap me back from distraction. The only way I could stop myself from going down that road was by telling myself everything would be okay. I had no idea what "okay" meant. I just decided that whatever happened, everything would work out. It was my way of controlling the uncontrollable.

If work was my salvation, weekends were a living hell. Once Thursday rolled around, I began dreading the weekends. There was nothing I feared more than the prospect of being stranded alone with my thoughts or the kids without anything to distract me. So I made sure I never was. I booked myself up obsessively and entertained constantly. It was easier for me to entertain than to be alone. Friday nights were the worst. Pat had always come in from the road on Fridays, and that had always been our night to reconnect. Once the kids were in bed, we listened to music and caught up with each other's lives. After his heart attack, I hosted barbecues on Friday nights. Saturdays and Sundays I organized outings with other moms and their kids or had them over for the afternoon. I always made sure to have people around. Saturday nights I invited my girlfriends over on a rotating basis. If one wasn't available that weekend, I moved on to the next. Sometimes one of our couple friends hosted a birthday dinner for a spouse on a Saturday night. Initially I dropped by for drinks, but I couldn't bear to be the only single person, so after a while I looked for ways to avoid those invitations.

At the end of April, Dr. Jane called a meeting. When we were seated, she showed me a printout of an MRI scan. "This is an image of a normally functioning brain," she said. "See how some of the areas of the brain are lighter and some are darker? With a brain that is functioning normally, you can see lighter and darker areas. The darker areas signify brain activity. When a brain has been damaged, the damaged areas appear grey." Then she showed me another printout of an MRI. "This is an image of Pat's brain," she said. The image was completely grey. There wasn't one dark area.

"Lisa," she said, "I'm sorry. I have nothing left to try. I know how hard that is for you to hear. You have been Patrick's greatest champion. You have done more for him than most people would have done. You can put your head on your pillow at night knowing that you did everything you possibly could for him. But you have a life to live, too, and you have to get on with living it. It's time for you to think about letting him go." Then she told me she was sending him back to Joseph Brant.

CHAPTER **TEN**

Deep End Here I Come

AFTER THE MEETING with Dr. Jane, I carried on. I went to work. I went to the hospital. I looked after the kids. To the outside world, it appeared as if nothing had changed. But inside, everything had changed. There weren't going to be any miracles. In one twenty-minute meeting the last vestiges of my hope for Pat's recovery had been extinguished. Until he died, or I came to terms with letting him go, we were both condemned to live in limbo. Until then, all I could do was put one foot in front of the other. So that is what I did.

Many times in life we have to just focus on putting one foot in front of the other in order to keep us moving forward when we are facing our fears, no matter how big or small they seem to be. That is what happened to me back in March 2003, when I was a director and the girls were five, three and eighteen months (Jack hadn't shown up yet). I came to work one Monday morning and my assistant told me the president wanted to see me in his office. It wasn't totally unusual for the president to call. Sometimes he asked me down to his office to solicit my opinion about this or that; other times he popped by my office to do the same. He was extremely approachable, but on such occasions I couldn't help feeling that he was testing me, and since I wasn't sure what was on his mind that day, I was a bit nervous as I headed down to his office.

When I walked in, he greeted me cordially and asked me to sit down. "Congratulations, Lisa," he said. "You're the next VP of sales, marketing and corporate communications."

I was so stunned, all I could do was stare at him open-mouthed. Eventually I managed to squeak out a few words. "Sales?" I said. "You're giving me sales? You realize my area's marketing. I've never sold a thing in my life."

"I'm obviously aware of that, Lisa," he smiled. "But I have no doubt you'll do a fantastic job."

I left his office in a state of shock. This wasn't just another step up. It was a quantum leap. No other promotion before or since has ever been as daunting. I'd come up through marketing. All my previous promotions had involved navigating a new region of a landscape whose contours were fundamentally familiar to me. But sales? I knew virtually nothing about sales. What's more, I'd be joining ranks with a handful of the most senior people in the company and reporting directly to the president. I was, to put it mildly, petrified.

When I told the president I'd never sold a thing in my life, I wasn't kidding. What I didn't tell him was that I was the world's worst negotiator. I always felt too sorry for the person on the other side. When Patrick and I used to go on vacation to Antigua, I always told him to give the souvenir guy whatever he wanted. As marketing director, I'd had to understand the revenue strategy side of sales, but the prospect of participating in a heated, possibly confrontational negotiation where I had to knock a percentage off the selling price to close a deal was way beyond my comfort zone. Of all the unknowns I was facing, that one terrified me the most.

I had no idea how much hands-on negotiating I'd actually have to do in the job, but I knew I'd be involved developing sales strategies on the customer side, so even if I never found myself face-to-face with a customer, I'd still need to grasp basic negotiating principles. And I'd have to lead the charge for a battalion of salespeople who made their living closing deals. Unless I had a firm grasp of what they went through every day, how could I possibly lead them?

It would have been so easy for me turn down that job. To tell my boss that it wasn't the right fit. Or I had too much going on in my life. With three kids under five, no one would have batted an eye. But you're not always ready when opportunity knocks. And big ambitions demand big risks. So saying no didn't even cross my mind.

The first thing I did when I learned I had the job was call several other FedEx vice-presidents of sales in the U.S. and ask for their advice. I told them I had no sales experience and would sincerely appreciate the chance to pick their brains. Could they walk me through their first ninety days on the job? I may have been green, but I was determined to learn, and what I lacked in expertise I made up for with the sheer force of my will. Since my determination to demystify the process and acquire as much intelligence as I could before taking over trumped any embarrassment I may have felt about appearing hopelessly naïve, I wasn't afraid to ask the most rudimentary questions. I asked what they'd done that had worked well, what they wished they'd done differently, and what significant challenges they'd faced, particularly during their first year.

Everybody I contacted was exceedingly generous with their time and expertise. People are usually flattered if you ask them to share their knowledge, although I'm sure some of the people I called must have been wondering how on earth I got the job without any sales experience. Still, admitting my ignorance gave me access to a treasure trove of information.

They told me to make sure I continued to meet regularly with my staff on a one-on-one basis after I met with them initially, and to make sure that I met with people at the level below those who reported to me directly. They were out in the field more. I'd pick up good ideas from them that I wouldn't hear about otherwise.

Those calls were absolutely essential in helping me formulate my plan for the first ninety days. They also helped carry me through my first year in the job. They buoyed my confidence, reinforced my belief that it was okay not to have all the answers and reminded me that admitting your vulnerabilities and asking for help is always a better strategy than trying to fake it or bluster your way through.

People often think it's too complicated to embark on a self-directed learning program to tackle a foreign business area. But you don't have to be a brainiac or MBA to master a new field. If you're motivated to learn, anyone can read, observe and ask questions to expand their knowledge. I'm living proof.

WHEN I WAS APPOINTED head of sales, my inner voice taunted me so loudly I was sure it had a megaphone. The majority of the sales force was male. Most of its members had ten or fifteen years of sales experience under their belts, and every single one knew I'd never closed a deal in my life. I had to sit in meetings with my team and try to win over people who were skeptically eagle-eyeing my every move. For my inner voice, it was a golden opportunity, and I assure you that it lost no time trying to undermine my confidence. I was convinced that the entire sales force was thinking one thing: *She's* running sales? She's a marketing girl. What the hell does she know about sales?

During my first year in the sales job, the reverb from my self-doubt was deafening, but I was determined not to let my inner voice win. So I dialed down the negative volume, dialed up the positive, and gave myself a good talking to. I decided there was absolutely no benefit to spending all my time worrying about what my sales force thought of me. So what if I didn't have sales experience? I'd figure it out. If I'd made it to the VP level in eleven years, I had to be doing something right. Besides, my boss thought I had what it took to do the job. He said he wasn't worried about my lack of sales experience. He believed a strong leader could always master a new business area, while an experienced candidate with weak leadership skills was unlikely to learn leadership skills on the job. Until I mustered some self-confidence, I'd have to rely on his confidence in me. In the meantime, I'd focus on the unique skills I *could* bring to the job.

What I could bring was my emotional intelligence. I was a good listener. I had empathy. I wasn't afraid to ask questions. I had strong communication skills, a knack for seeing the big picture and the ability to collaborate, motivate and inspire. Maybe most importantly, I wasn't afraid to admit what I didn't know. Once I started focusing on my strengths instead of my doubts, I realized I had a lot more going for me than I'd initially thought.

My little pep talk worked. I'm not saying that I never heard from my doubting inner voice again. It was persistent, I'll give it that. But whenever it started up, I beat it back with a stick, and I never allowed it to gain the upper hand again. After all, if you can't convince yourself you can do the impossible, how can you possibly convince anyone else?

Some people think their careers will unfold in an orderly fashion. But if you surveyed people, I think most would tell you they didn't wind up following the career path they'd mapped out for themselves. It's wise to plan your career path, of course. But you can't get locked into it. You have to be willing to zig and zag.

Looking back, I think the biggest takeaway from the sales job was that you don't always see career opportunities coming. And because you don't, you don't plan to go in that direction. My boss offered me the job because he saw certain capacities in me that I didn't see in myself. I think mentors often see something in you that you don't see in yourself. A lot of people are thrown if an opportunity comes along that doesn't fit the paradigm they've envisioned for themselves, so they pass it up. But if an opportunity comes running to find you, you can't run for cover in the opposite direction. No matter how much it terrifies you, you have to swallow your fears and tell yourself you're going to kick ass.

Of course if you manage to silence your doubting inner voice once, it becomes much easier to silence it the next time. A few years later, when I made another lateral move and had to manage hourly employees and essentially start from scratch again, I didn't find it nearly as daunting to show my inner voice who was boss. By then, I'd developed the habit of tuning it out. But by then I also had a proven track record of knowing zero about an area of the business and making it a success with my team.

IN THE PREVIOUS CHAPTER I talked about how writing down your goals can help make them a reality. The idea that you can turn thought into action in many different circumstances isn't just some loosey-goosey one: if you have a specific goal, your goal is within reason, you picture it clearly and make visualization a habit, substantial evidence exists that you can accomplish much more than if you didn't take those steps. There's a reason the theme keeps popping up in motivational books. It works!

Visualization has helped many successful people achieve their goals. However, you can't just close your eyes, think happy thoughts and expect Tinkerbell to show up, sprinkle you with fairy dust and take you to Neverland. It takes a lot of hard work and discipline to accomplish any goal worth achieving.

Even though I know visualization works, and consider it to be one of the driving forces behind my business success, I find it fascinating to read about others who have used it successfully. Natan Sharansky is a computer specialist who spent nine years in Soviet prisons during the 1970s and 1980s after being accused of spying for the United States. Sharanksy was a chess prodigy. When he was in solitary confinement, he spent his time mentally playing chess against himself in order to maintain his sanity. During those solitary matches, he set himself the goal of becoming the world chess champion. Years after he was released from prison, he beat the reigning world chess champion, Gary Kasparov. That story sounds as if it was ripped from the pages of *Ripley's Believe It Or Not!*, but it's true.

While it has been widely known for years that visualization works, thanks to neural imaging, we now know why it does. When we visualize, our brain cells actually interpret visualization as a real-life action and prime the body to behave in the way that our imagination wants it to behave. In other words, the visualization process sends a message to our brain that we're on a mission and starts training it to work towards our goal. It's as if we had a personal trainer inside our own mind. The process also jumpstarts our creativity by opening doorways to resources in our brain that have been shoved away in dusty corners for years.

I talked earlier about how I pictured fitting into my favourite jeans to lose weight after my pregnancies. I've learned that if I can picture myself achieving a goal, I not only push myself harder to achieve it, but I have a much clearer picture of the baby steps I have to take to get there. Before I deliver a speech, for instance, I visualize myself standing at the podium, imagine the looks on the audience's faces, and the crowd's reaction when I'm done. If I don't picture myself killing it, chances are I won't. But the real beauty of visualization is that it's such a versatile tool. You never know when it will come in handy.

In 2012, I participated in an episode of *Undercover Boss Canada*. When I signed on to do the show, I told the director, who'd directed other episodes of the series, "Just so you know, this is going to be the best episode you've ever directed. It's going to win an award." He reminded me of my prediction the night we attended the Canadian Screen Awards and the show won for Best Direction.

And remember how I mentioned that Pat and I decided to live at home before we were married so we could save for a house? Well, shortly before we were married, we bought a house on the lake in Burlington. I loved that little house. It had loads of character and it stood on a huge lot with beautiful old trees. But it was a first house — it had likely been a cottage at one point — and I knew we'd soon outgrow it.

Shortly after Hailey was born, Pat and I went to a party at a friend's place in Millcroft, a golf community in north Burlington. I fell in love with that house the first time I saw it. It was a lovely two-storey, four-bedroom with a peaked roof and wraparound porch that stood on a corner lot backing onto a golf course.

The moment I laid eyes on it I told Pat it would be ours one day. He just laughed. First, it wasn't for sale. Second, we couldn't possibly afford it. But I had other ideas. I told our friend that if he ever decided to sell we wanted to buy, and from that moment on I began envisioning the house as ours.

I decorated it in my head, imagined the renovations we'd do, parties we'd throw, movies we'd watch as a family and summer afternoons we'd sit on the patio inhaling the scent of freshly mown grass wafting our way from the golf course. I kept those images in my mind, savoured them regularly and never let doubt cloud my vision.

A couple of years later our friend called to say he was ready to sell. Were we interested? By then the stars had aligned. We were expecting our second child, our first house had risen considerably in value, and our friend's mother, who was a real estate agent, offered to waive her commission on the sale. "See, Pat," I said when the deal was done. "I told you the house would be ours one day."

AS I CLIMBED from manager to director to VP, I had to decide what kind of leader I was going to be. Finding your voice is one of the loveliest discoveries you will make as a leader. But finding it takes time. You have to observe other leadership styles, emulate the traits you admire, ignore the ones you don't and incorporate elements that are uniquely your own. The goal isn't imitation. It's finding the voice that's true to who you are.

Above all, your goal should be to formulate an authentic leadership style that plays to your strengths. If your strength is to be nurturing and empathic, then you have to let those qualities shine through. The worst thing you can do is hide the person you are or pretend to be someone you're not.

If you try to be aggressive because you think that's what's expected of you, you'll just wind up diminishing yourself and the qualities you have to offer. My own leadership style is governed by one guiding principle: Do unto others as you would have them do unto you. The Golden Rule may not be considered a cutting-edge management theory, but putting myself in other people's shoes and treating them the way I'd like to be treated has always worked for me.

I started thinking of The Golden Rule as the pillar of my leadership philosophy early in my career. As a novice, I had the great good fortune to work for a manager who showed tremendous trust in her team and who always canvassed others' opinions before making decisions. Under her tutelage, I learned that giving people the chance to participate in the decision-making process not only brought out the best in them; it empowered them and invariably improved the result. So right from the start I knew that I wanted to be an inclusive leader, and as I rose through the ranks, inclusivity became a key element of my style.

By the time I took on the sales job, I'd taken the idea of inclusivity to a whole new level. The first week on the job I walked into staff meetings with my pen and notebook in hand and said, "Okay guys. What's on your mind? Help me create my To Do List." Then I peppered my team with questions. I had three themes: What's working for you? What's bogging you down? What can I do to make your jobs easier? Gradually, I became known as the person who always asked her team for help with her To Do list. The approach became a hallmark of my style.

I spent the first three months listening, observing and enquiring. I spent one day a week in the office and the other four going out on sales calls with my reps across the country. Here's what I discovered: if you ask people to tell you what's on their minds, they're usually pretty happy to oblige, especially when they feel as if they've been beating their heads against a wall for a long time.

When I asked my team for their input, the floodgates opened. They told me that we weren't offering our customers aggressive enough discounts; as a result, the competition had the edge. They told me that they had to fill out so many forms for our internal approval process that they were losing valuable face time with customers — time they should rightly have been spending building client relationships and closing deals.

I spent the next three months coming up with a plan

to address the problems they said were hampering their ability to perform at an optimum level. I unveiled my plan at a sales rally. I stood onstage in front of a large screen in a hotel conference room and clicked on my first PowerPoint slide. It said "The Ten Demandments." "This is a list of ten problems you told me needed fixing," I said. Then I went down the list item by item. With each one, I said, "Here's your demand. Here's the solution. We'll have the solution in place by such-and-such a date." When I finished, I received a standing ovation. It was one of the most gratifying moments of my career.

I'd love to say I was a genius for taking the approach I did, but there was nothing genius about it. My method was simple and I didn't try to overcomplicate it. I just used my common sense. I assumed my staff knew more than I did, I asked for their input and I took what they told me seriously.

I believe that one's success as a leader is inextricably linked to the team's performance, and that you can't have one without the other. In my view, what distinguishes a boss from a leader is the ability to connect the dots between nurturing her team and achieving results. A leader listens to her team, empowers them and extends a helping hand when needed. A boss just barks orders.

At my company you're expected to be a team player. If you're not, you're considered an outlier. But every company can make a bad hire occasionally, and from time to time I encountered management types whose styles didn't jibe with our company's culture. Some were so hell-bent on getting ahead they spent all their time trying to shine the spotlight on themselves. They blindsided coworkers, called them out in meetings and deliberately let them founder in the belief that doing so would make them look better. Some acted as if nobody had anything to teach them. Either they were dismissive of anyone they didn't deem useful to their careers, or they had so little interest in collaboration they showed up to meetings without a notebook or pen. If you asked them a simple strategy question, they told you to worry about your own department. Needless to say their careers didn't go the way they'd planned.

In a million years it would never have occurred to me to behave that way. My natural impulse has always been to try to improve a situation by helping someone who's foundering, as I'd tried to help the Chuck E. Cheese's birthday hostesses who were struggling to stay on top of their tables. That's my impulse, because that's how I was raised — by my parents and by my company.

Earning your team's trust, loyalty and respect is a far better way to realize your ambitions than by alienating them. It all comes back to treating others the way you'd like to be treated. If you thwart instead of support and make it all about you instead of your team, that behaviour will come back to haunt you.

Another part of my repertoire as a leader is to give everyone the same time, attention and respect, regardless of their rank. As a novice, I sometimes crossed paths with superiors who had a much higher rank than I did. No matter what their rank, they always made me feel valued. They did it by treating me like one of their peers.

I always remembered that feeling and the message that

went with it: It doesn't matter what your job is, because every job counts. Your title defines your role in the company but not your value to it: it's what you do, not who you are. The power lies with the team, not the individual. Today, it doesn't matter who's in front of me. It could be one of my couriers or one of my VPs. I treat everyone the same way.

The idea that leaders should be visible, accessible and approachable, that a company culture requires constant nurturing and that it takes a village to make a company great permeates FedEx's culture from the top down. I was raised in that culture and absorbed its values. They profoundly shaped my thoughts on leadership and remain integral to the way I lead today.

A LOT OF LEADERS are afraid to hire someone who is smarter than they are. But one of the best pieces of advice I ever received from a mentor was that you don't get paid for what you do as a leader. You get paid for what your team does. Whenever others praised him for being such a great leader he'd say, "Look, the only smart thing I've done is hire people who are smarter than me." The brighter your team, the better you'll look. You get to bask in their reflected glory. So when I was in a position to hire, I surrounded myself with the smartest people I could find and I hired people whose skills complemented mine. I wanted diversity, not a mirror image.

But you can't micromanage "A players" or they'll leave.

Fortunately, it's never been my style to get into the weeds with my staff. I saw how demoralizing micromanagement was for others and I realized what a colossal time-waster it would be for me. I just tried to surround myself with the best people I could find and trust them to do their jobs until I had good reason not to. Probably the biggest disincentive, though, was that I'd have hated to be micromanaged myself.

A lot of leaders view their title as a signal that the waters should part when they enter the room. But the mentor who promoted me to the sales job taught me by example that your title isn't what defines you as a leader. What does is how you treat others.

He was always looking for ways to lend a hand. He never just gave you a target and told you to hit it. He viewed his title as a tool to help his team perform their jobs more effectively and always asked how he could help. And unlike a lot of bosses, he made you feel that it would be okay to tell him something he didn't want to hear, so you could go to him if you ran into trouble down the road. You couldn't just go into his office and dump your problems on his desk. That wasn't going to fly. But you could always seek his guidance. He had a way of making you feel that you were the most important person in the room. I learned so much about good leadership under his wing. The more I followed his lead and treated my title as an enabler to help my team, the better my team performed. The better they performed, the more I got noticed. Today I pass on the lessons he taught me to my own team.

AFTER I'D BEEN IN THE JOB for a few years, my boss came to me and said that the sales department had grown too large. He planned to make it its own department and create a new department by joining marketing and corporate communications with customer service, customer automation and global trade service. I could stay on as vice-president of the new sales department or take a lateral position and become vice-president of marketing, customer experience and corporate communications. He left it entirely up to me to decide.

I had many good reasons to stay exactly where I was. By then I had a firm handle on how to do the sales job and my team was achieving real results. What's more, a lateral move would definitely mean more work. The new job involved overseeing our customer service, clearance operations and IT automation, and I knew nothing about clearing packages or running a call centre. As for the IT automation part, while I'd had to oversee the content on our Canadian website as products and pricing manager, I didn't have a clue about website technology. If I took the promotion I'd have to master three new areas of the business that were utterly unfamiliar to me while continuing to handle the marketing and corporate communications pieces.

Ordinarily, I'd have turned to books to quell my fears. But books weren't going to save me this time. There were only a few around on how to run a call centre and none on how to run a successful clearance operation. Nor was it going to be much help to talk to vice-presidents who ran clearance operations in the other global regions, since every government had its own customs requirements. For the first time in my career I'd be out there on my own. The only way I could learn the job was by spending time with my team, observing operations and asking questions.

To make matters even more interesting, for the first time in my career I'd also have to manage hourly employees. So if I accepted the promotion, in addition to all the other demands of the job I'd have to completely rethink my management approach, particularly with respect to the style and content of my communications.

What's more, by the time that opportunity arose, our family had expanded again — Jack had arrived in 2004, two years after I became a VP. We'd hired Jojo when Mya was six months old, but even with her help and my parents on speed dial, our lives required complicated logistics to keep the trains running on time. But I remembered my mentor's advice about broadening my skills whenever I had the chance, and once again, I said yes.

When it comes to risk-taking, my mom is my role model. When I was old enough to understand, she told me she was scared to leave her marriage, but after she'd summoned the courage, she discovered she had more strength than she knew. I've often wondered about what my life would have been like if she'd stayed in an unhappy marriage. I can't know of course, but I doubt I'd be the person I am today. My dad wasn't happy with her decision and neither was I. But her risk freed us both up to lead happier, more fulfilling lives. My mom taught me by example that no matter how scared you are, facing your fears is always better than running from them. If you're not willing to take risks, you'll get what you settle for. When my mom took that step to leave her marriage, she set in motion events that led her to find the person with whom I believe she was meant to share her life, and she liberated my dad to find the person with whom I believe he was meant to share his. Looking back, I think when I saw both parents so happy in their new relationships, and two new families grow from the seeds of that happiness — I decided that some relationships are meant to be and others are not. If you're willing to risk taking a step towards the future you long for but cannot see, the benefits will cascade outward in every direction.

It comes down to deciding how you want to live your life. In my view there are basically two ways to go: you can either live your life to the fullest or you can settle for the life you've got. But if you choose to settle and remain unhappy, you're not really living. You're just existing.

Fear is a thief. It will rob you of joy, opportunity and, if you allow it, ultimately of life itself. I know so many women who stay in unhappy marriages out of fear — fear that they won't be able to support themselves, fear that their lifestyles will diminish, fear that their kids will suffer. But as hard as it is to face your fears, I believe if you've done everything you possibly can to fix a problem and it persists, staying mired in misery is worse.

Some people think their kids will have an easier time of it if they delay splitting until the kids are older. But I don't think there's any good time for a child to find out that their parents are divorcing. And I think children can sense their parents' unhappiness at any age. They can tell whether their parents delight in each other's company or are leading separate lives and living as roommates under the same roof. They know because they're little sponges.

If a marriage is beyond repair, then sooner or later it's going to sink. When it does, people are going to get hurt. Staying for the children's sake, or telling yourself that that's the reason you're staying, when what's really holding you back are your fears, doesn't serve anyone's interests.

Every marriage is unique, as unique as our set of fingerprints. So, too, are the factors that determine the decision to stay or leave. But I can't say that I've ever met an unhappily married woman who regretted leaving her marriage. I've only met women who say they wish they'd left sooner.

When I'm contemplating taking a risk, I always try to imagine the worst-case scenario. If I can live with it, I go for it. If I can't, I don't. Often the worst-case scenario is that I'll screw up and embarrass myself. But that's a risk I'm willing to take. Whatever happens, I figure eventually I'll land on my feet, and if I do embarrass myself, at least I tried. Besides, people respect a risk-taker. If you try, but you fall on your face, most people will cut you slack. Besides, you know what they say: no guts, no glory.

WITH FOUR CHILDREN and two increasingly demanding careers, Pat and I struggled to achieve equilibrium between our work and family lives. We hoped to find a perfect balance between the two. We actually thought we'd achieve it. Of course we never did. Most days, controlled chaos was the best we could hope for.

Eventually I came to the conclusion that chasing that elusive ideal was an unrealistic goal. Balance implies a perfect state of being — one you can attain if only you find the right formula. Maybe some people achieve balance for a while, but I don't think they sustain it for very long. I've certainly never managed to do so, and I don't know anyone who has.

That's why I strive less for balance than for ebb and flow. I have intense periods of work and intense periods of relaxation. Sometimes my life is crazy busy; sometimes it's less so. Mostly I just try to be fully present wherever I am. When I'm at work, my head's in my work. When I'm with my kids, my attention is focused on them. When I'm with my friends, I'm with my friends and when I'm with myself, I focus on me.

How do I manage to achieve an ebb and flow? By making a conscious effort to live in the moment and by working hard to develop a discipline around the practice. Some people are so addicted to checking their phone messages when they're on vacation they can't even part with them for an afternoon. They're sitting at the beach a thousand miles from home, but they might as well be at the office because that's where their heads are. When I'm on vacation, I've learned to unplug. I can't go off the grid entirely, but I've learned to do a quick check in the morning and at the end of the day.

At first it wasn't easy to let go. I had to wean myself from the habit of constantly checking my messages. But I trained myself to do it because I wanted to spend that time with my kids. Another area I'm really trying to work on as a parent is remembering to focus on what's important in the moment. My son is still at an age where he likes me to tuck him in on the nights when I'm home. Once he's in bed, he calls from upstairs to say he's ready. Before, if I was doing a bit of work downstairs and was in mid-email, my inclination was to say, "Okay, buddy, be there in a few minutes." But inevitably a few minutes stretched into ten or fifteen, and by the time I'd made it upstairs he was asleep. I enjoy the ritual of tucking my son in, and I know I'm only going to get a finite number of nights when he still wants me to do it and those nights are vanishing quickly. So now I go the moment he calls me. When my kids need to talk with me, I make a conscious effort to stop and give them my undivided attention regardless of what I'm doing at the time. When I'm home, I try not to respond to emails unless they're absolutely necessary. I don't always succeed, but I always try. If I slip, as I did when Jack called me to tuck him in, I catch myself and vow to do better tomorrow.

Just as you need self-awareness to be a good parent, you need it to be an effective leader. At least your kids won't be shy about telling you when you're falling down on the job. But nobody wants to tell their boss the truth. That's why it's doubly important for you to learn how to tell it to yourself.

I still live my life in a state of controlled chaos. But the less I strive for balance and the more I strive for ebb and flow and view work and family as complementary, as opposed to conflicting, forces in my life, the more contented I feel.

If you have kids, you can't just devote all your spare energy to them. You have to take time for yourself, and for your partner if you have one. When Pat and I were in the thick of it during the career-building years of our thirties, we made a concerted effort to focus on each other as often as we possibly could. During that period of our lives, our marriage mirrored the relationship we'd forged in high school. I continued to take the lead in most matters, and he continued to let me. While he happily followed my lead, he often said that he wished I needed him more. I think he felt underemployed in our marriage in that way. But I didn't look to Pat to be my mentor. I just loved him.

He was still a director when I made VP, but he had ambitions to move up as well, so at night when I came home he always wanted to pick my brain about how I'd handled situations at work that day. I was exhausted. I just wanted to park my day. But Pat was never too tired to learn. He was always trying to improve himself. He loved listening to Tony Robbins tapes. I think he had them all.

When I think back on all the conscious choices I made that helped me succeed, by far the smartest was marrying a man who wasn't threatened by my success. Pat was a competitive guy. He liked to win at business, in Vegas and at golf. But he never competed with me. When I was a VP, I earned a lot more money than he did, but he couldn't have cared less. He was always just proud of me. He used to tell his customers I was going to be president one day. You'll see, he'd say. She's going to run that company one day.

At home, we operated as a team. Our motto was "divide and conquer." Given my natural talents as a planner and organizer I willingly assumed the role of household manager. Otherwise, we split responsibilities down the middle. We cooked together, shared the shopping, chores and duties around the kids. On weekends, he made breakfast and took the girls to dance. He dressed them in their tutus, drove them to classes and hung out with the moms at Tim Hortons until classes were over. He could make a better ballet bun than most of the moms.

There was just one problem: he was on the road a lot. When Hailey was born, he had a job as a sales agent for a stone supplier and he started going on the road to service his customers two or three weeks a month. He was home on weekends, but for the first four years and two kids — until Mya was born and we hired Jojo — there were many days when I felt like a single parent. If one of the kids got sick when he was out of town, that extra stress factor pushed me right over the edge.

It wasn't long before I started resenting him for being away so much, and resenting his boss for making him travel all the time. I began complaining about the situation non-stop. I started pressuring him to get another job. His answer was always the same: "What do you want me to do? There isn't a sales job in the world that doesn't involve travel."

When Pat was out of town he used to call me from his hotel room at night to ask how my day was going. When he called, I knew he'd just enjoyed a leisurely dinner with his customers and once we hung up the phone he planned to settle in to watch a movie. At such times, I wasn't inclined to say, "Things are great, honey. Thanks for calling. Glad you're having such a wonderful time." I was inclined to say, "How do you think my day was, Pat? Work was crazy busy, Chloe's sick, we're out of milk, and I still have about five hours of work ahead of me." Or, "How was *my* day? Are you freaking *kidding* me? Where do I start? One of us is going to have to quit our job or I'll lose my mind."

I kept this up for quite a while. I was a broken record, really. But my complaining wasn't solving anything. All it was doing was causing friction between us. Eventually it occurred to me that I must have sounded so resentful when he called that he was probably holding the phone away from his ear. I hated his travel schedule. But I also hated being a nagging wife and I really didn't want to be that person, so I realized I had two choices: I could continue to blame Pat for having a job that took him away so much and let my resentments fester. Or I could do what my great-grandmother had advised: accept my reality and try to find something positive about it.

If his travel schedule wasn't going to change, then I had to. In theory, that idea made sense. In practice, it was ridiculous to think that I could just flick a switch in my head and get rid of all my resentment. Still, I kept circling back to the idea that demonizing Pat wasn't the answer. I had to engineer an attitude adjustment. But how?

I started wondering if maybe there was some way to apply the techniques I'd learned to overcome obstacles at work to surmounting this obstacle in my marriage. I decided to try using logic to attack the problem, the way I did to resolve problems at work. I told myself that Patrick had a job he loved, at which he excelled and for which he was well paid. I reminded myself that when he was home, he was a wonderful hands-on dad. Maybe instead of complaining that he had to find another job, I should start thinking about what my life would be like if he had a job he hated. Or if he took another job just to make me happy. It wasn't much of a stretch to imagine how resentful he'd be then. Next, I asked myself how I'd feel if he lost the job he had and I had to become the sole provider. Suddenly a whole new range of possibilities presented themselves, all more sobering than the one I was facing.

The strategy worked. Instead of focusing on what was wrong with my life, I decided to focus on what was good about it. Once I made that mental shift, I realized I actually had a lot to feel grateful for. I'm not saying all my resentment suddenly evaporated. Some days it really bothered me that Pat wasn't around when I needed him. But I no longer dwelled on them. Still, the only reason I was able to make that adjustment was because I knew I had a partner who would have been just as willing to make that adjustment for me if the situation had been reversed. If only one person is making sacrifices for the marriage's greater good, it will never work.

AS DEVOUTLY AS I PLAN, I'm also a big believer in embracing spontaneity whenever possible. I realized early on, however, that hoping spontaneity would just happen out of the blue wasn't going to cut it as a strategic plan. If I wanted to have an adult conversation with Pat, the only way I was going to achieve that goal was by orchestrating the conditions for spontaneity to happen. So orchestrate I did. If I hadn't seen him in a week or couldn't bear the thought of cooking one more meal (and I was able to arrange babysitting), I called him and told him to meet me for dinner.

If I hadn't been intentional about those plans, they probably wouldn't have happened. Here's what would have happened instead: Pat would have been tired. I'd have been tired. We'd have gone home to another night of chaos, ordered a pizza, put the kids to bed and fallen face forward into bed ourselves.

I probably organized the majority of those date nights, but I wasn't the only spontaneity enforcer in our marriage. Pat and I both understood the importance of carving out time for one another; we both knew that finding that time wouldn't happen by chance, and we both took responsibility for making it happen. Some nights I walked in the door exhausted only to find that Pat had returned from a business trip early that day, dropped the kids at my parents and made us a candlelit dinner.

If my parents were willing to cover, sometimes we even escaped to our friends' cottage for the weekend. We also joined each other on business trips whenever possible. It would have been much easier for me to tell Pat I couldn't get away. To say it would be far too complicated to rearrange my schedule. But when life is hurtling by, it's so easy to lose track of one another. We found a way.

If I didn't have parents who were willing to cover at a moment's notice or a nanny who was willing to work overtime, it would obviously have been much tougher for us to catch a break. But I still think I'd have found a way. If you want to breathe, the only way I've ever found to make that happen is by making breathing a priority.

I CAN'T POSSIBLY TALK about how I manage my life without discussing my lists. I wouldn't be able to function without them. I already told you about my goal lists. But I have two other master lists that I carry with me at all times. One is for everything I have to remember for work; the other is for things I have to remember around the house and kids. I write everything down on one of those lists, and I do it as soon as it pops into my head. Otherwise, I'll forget. Like furnace filters. I'd definitely forget to buy furnace filters.

At the start of every week, I look at my two master lists, decide what I have to do that week and transfer those items to two weekly lists I also carry with me. Everything I have to accomplish for that week goes on one of those two lists. On a good week, I can knock fifteen items off my master lists.

In addition to my two goal lists and my two master task lists, and my two weekly task lists, I also record all the important dates I need to have at my fingertips in the calendar in my Day-Timer. I write down birthdays, travel dates, insurance renewal dates, due dates for my house taxes and so on. Let's say the renewal date for Pat's driver's licence was coming up. I marked down that date and when I saw it was coming up I reminded him to take care of the renewal.

Some women would think I was nuts for taking on my husband's to-do list on top of everything else I had going on. But I didn't see it as a burden. I like taking care of people, and I was already making the list so it was no big deal to enter his dates. But to be honest, I did it as much for me as for him. I knew he'd forget to renew his insurance and I'm such a rule-follower that I didn't want him to get stopped by the police, although I'm not sure why I was so worried. He'd probably have charmed his way out of a ticket.

I realize it would be more efficient to keep track of my life on my iPhone. But I'm a highly visual person and writing things out helps me absorb and remember information. Besides, I enjoy the weekly ritual of writing out my lists. It gives me a sense of control over my life, even if that sense is largely illusory.

But it doesn't really matter what system you use to keep track of your life, as long as it helps you stay organized. If you're organized, you'll reduce your stress level and free up your brain to focus on more important matters. Once you write things down, you don't have to worry about forgetting them. You can cross worrying off your list.

MAKING LISTS HELPED keep me on top of my daily tasks and commitments; unfortunately it didn't alleviate the profound anxiety and stress I experienced after Pat got sick. One of the ways I found to manage then was learning how to meditate. Meditation is in vogue now. You can download meditation apps and every day I come across another article about CEOs who've incorporated the practice into their daily routines. But back then, very few people I knew were familiar with it.

Learning to meditate did not come easily to me. In fact, it's one of the hardest skills I have ever tried to master. Even under normal circumstances, quieting your mind is a hard thing to do. And there was nothing normal about my circumstances. It took me a good year before I started to reap any benefits from the practice at all. Throughout that year I wanted to give up so many times. But eventually I began to notice that I felt calmer, had more patience and control and could get to a place of serenity faster.

Of all the strategies I found to help me during that terrible time, meditation was the most beneficial — so much so that I've incorporated it into my daily routine. Today, I take time to clear my head on a daily basis. I take that time personally and professionally and I'm extremely disciplined about taking it. It's my opportunity to step back, pause and reflect, breathe and regroup. I couldn't function without it.

I meditate every morning, when the kids are still asleep. It's my only quiet time. On a good day I can meditate for fifteen and sometimes even twenty minutes. But even ten minutes is useful. Once I meditate, I'm refreshed and ready to start my day.

At night, I'll take a moment after I turn out the lights to reflect on my day and think about whether there was anything I could have done differently. Maybe I was impatient with one of my kids. Maybe I became overly involved with a work issue that I should have let my management team handle. If so, I make a note to myself to try to do better next time.

At work, I make sure to block off three hours a week and leave that time as white space on my calendar. Every week, come hell or high water, I shut my office door and use that time to think about what has gone well during that week and what could have gone better, to set my goals for the coming week, decide what steps I'll take towards achieving them, reflect on where my life is at that moment and where I'd like it to go.

I often share this routine with my audiences when I speak. When I do, you'd think I'd handed them one of the secrets of the universe. One time a lawyer emailed me afterwards to say that simply clearing her deck for a few hours a week and using that time to reflect on her goals had resulted in her taking concrete action towards achieving them. She'd started building her legacy, hired a designer to create a website and a writer to conduct interviews for her forthcoming book. She also wrote that she was determined to pay the message forward, which I loved.

I'm equally vigilant about taking time-outs to recharge my batteries at home, too, even if I only take a few hours a week to read a book or sip a cup of tea and stare at a wall. I have so many demands coming at me from all quarters that if I don't close up shop once in a while and hang out a Gone Fishing sign, I simply couldn't cope. I think of those interludes as power naps for my brain. I tell the kids

I'm going upstairs to my room for a while to read and rest my brain and they're not to knock on the door or text me. They know to leave me alone unless the house is on fire. I know some women who don't even allow themselves an hour to relax in the bath without interruptions. But I'm deliberate about those moments because they're precious to me. And because I've learned you never know when you'll get another one.

CHAPTER ELEVEN

Letting Go

DURING THE MONTHS AT CHEDOKE, I'd continued to be haunted by all the questions that had plagued me since the night Pat collapsed. But after he'd been in rehab for a few months without any sign of improvement, I was tormented by another question: Why isn't my visualizing working? From the moment the doctors gave me Pat's prognosis I'd visualized a miracle. Then I'd done everything I'd always done to achieve my goal. I'd pictured it, worked diligently to make it happen and refused to entertain doubts that I couldn't. I'd followed all the rules that had brought me so much success in my career. But after nine months, I had nothing to show for my efforts. That wasn't how it was supposed to work.

In October 2007, when I'd learned that Pat had been accepted into Chedoke, I'd had so much confidence in his recovery I'd told the nurses at Joe Brant he'd come back and high five them all. Now I was returning with him on a stretcher and the news that there wasn't any hope. The prospect of facing those nurses was almost more than I could bear. For nine months I'd told the world that Pat would get a miracle. For nine months I'd held fast to that vision. During that time I'd lowered my expectations about the kind of miracle to expect, but I'd never stopped believing one would come to pass. When I saw that MRI, I knew he was going back to Joseph Brant to die.

When Pat went back to Joseph Brant, I plunged into the deepest despair I had experienced since my ordeal began. A few weeks after he returned, I was sitting in his room on the Saturday of the May long weekend. As I gazed out the window watching the sailboats drifting by on Lake Ontario and the people strolling by on the sidewalks below, my mind began to wander. I thought about what other people were doing that weekend. I pictured parents pushing their kids on swings and families opening their cottages for the season. I thought about how our family should be out enjoying the nice weather, too; instead, I was sitting in a hospital room on a glorious day with a husband who'd been given no hope for a meaningful life. Then my mind leapt forward to how he wouldn't be around for the kids' graduations and weddings and I started worrying about how Jack was going to grow up without a father and who was going take him to his hockey games and teach him how to tie a tie, and I started spiraling into a black hole. Unless I stopped thinking about what had been and was never going to be, I'd go mad. But how could I stop my mind from circling backwards and forwards to that dark place? The only way I could imagine turning off the movie playing in my head was by training my mind to focus on what was directly in front of me — and what was directly in front of me were the next twenty-four hours. From that moment on, I only allowed myself to think about those hours. As soon as my mind began to drift backwards or forwards, I consciously stopped myself from going down those roads. Many days I didn't succeed. Many days I railed at fate and sobbed that I wanted my life back. But the more I made an effort to narrow my gaze, the less I skidded into despair.

In the absence of hope, I needed something else to keep me going. After Pat went back to Joseph Brant, I hit upon the idea of bringing him home for Sunday visits. I'd been dragging the kids to see Pat every Sunday and they'd begun to chafe at the visits. Since Pat was now on a medical floor, it occurred to me that if I could bring him home on Sundays, seeing their dad wouldn't have to feel like an obligation for the kids. They could spend time with him without interruption to their lives. I'd get a break from the hospital as well, and for one day a week we'd have some degree of normalcy as a family. I couldn't see a downside.

I fully expected the authorities to say no when I raised the idea. If you ask people to try something that's never been done before, they'll almost always tell you why it can't be done. Saying no is easy. Saying yes takes much more effort. And at first, no was the answer the staff gave me, partly because they had several legitimate safety concerns, and partly because preparing Pat to leave the hospital by noon involved a lot of extra work for them. They only had a skeleton staff working on the weekends. If other patients needed immediate attention, they could deal with Pat whenever they had the time, and they feared losing that flexibility in their schedules. But I was determined to turn a no into a yes because yes was the answer I needed. I agreed to meet all of their medical requirements. I promised to stick to a set schedule every week. I addressed all of their outstanding concerns about why the plan couldn't work. I reminded them how much bringing Pat home would mean to us as a family.

Pat came home for the first time in June. I'm not sure why the staff agreed to let him go. Maybe they saw how hard I was fighting. Maybe they felt sorry for me. Maybe I just wore them down. In any event, I arranged for a wheelchair taxi to pick him up at noon and he stayed until four.

The visit went off without a hitch. For the next nine months he came home virtually every Sunday. Sunday became an oasis in my week. I'd be in the kitchen making dinner and he'd be in his wheelchair beside me and the stereo would be playing and the kids would come flying downstairs and say "Hi Dad" on their way out the door. Sometimes I wheeled him out to the patio. Seeing him sitting outside with the sun on his face made my heart soar. Sometimes when the kids were horsing around in the pool they asked if they could splash him. From time to time I'd come downstairs to find Mya chattering away to him in the kitchen. Having him home was bittersweet, too, of course, since his presence was a constant reminder of everything we'd lost. But the sweetness far outweighed the sorrow. For those few hours a week his presence allowed us to feel whole as a family.

During those months I took comfort wherever I could find it. One place I found it was in Dr. Jane's words that I could put my head on my pillow at night knowing I'd done everything I possibly could have for Pat. I also took solace in the knowledge that he wasn't in any physical pain.

When you spend as much time in hospitals as I did, you witness a great deal of suffering; no matter how profound your own suffering, you can't help but notice that there's always someone else whose suffering is worse. At one point, Pat shared a room with a man who'd been stricken with ALS. ALS is a ravaging disease. It causes your muscles to waste away. First you can't walk, then you can't speak, then you can't breathe. But its most perverse cruelty is that it doesn't affect your brain. Not only are you fully aware that eventually you'll suffocate; you have to endure the agony in slow motion. I used to sit in Pat's room and think about how that poor man had a perfect mind but a body that was betraying him while my husband lay in the next bed with a perfect body and no mind. If Pat had to suffer one of those two fates, I knew which one I'd choose.

The months wore on. By then, I'd been living with an incapacitated husband for so long that people sometimes forgot how different my life was from theirs. Occasionally

I'd be out with my girlfriends and they'd start complaining about their husbands' annoying habits. It was just girl talk. Before Pat fell ill, I'd probably have rolled my eyes in commiseration. But now an unbridgeable gulf existed between us. Sometimes I let their comments go. But sometimes I said, "I'm the wrong person for you to be complaining to." They were horrified at their gaffe and apologized profusely. But at such moments I felt deeply alone.

Sometimes, though, the opposite happened. Sometimes a colleague would tell me how she'd started to become upset about some trivial matter in her day but then remembered what I was dealing with and regained perspective. I found those stories uplifting. They made me feel that even though Patrick's life was pretty much gone, the tragedy of his life was inspiring others to value their own lives more.

NOT LONG AFTER PAT RETURNED to Joe Brant, I received a call from one of Pat's close friends. They'd known each other since high school. He said he had something important to discuss with me and wanted to come by. As soon as I opened the door I could see that he was an emotional wreck. When we sat down, he said he'd agonized for months about coming to me, but had finally decided that he couldn't keep silent anymore.

He proceeded to tell me that one night when he and Pat had gone out for a beer, Pat had asked him for a favour: "If, for whatever reason, I wind up in a vegetative state, don't let Lisa keep me alive."

He said he'd spent many sleepless nights since Pat's heart attack wrestling with whether to tell me about his request, but after Pat came out of rehab and the doctors said there was nothing more they could do for him, he finally decided to speak to me. "Lisa," he said. "He doesn't want to live this way. You have to let him go."

His revelation stunned me. It wasn't just that it was so hard for me to hear what he had to say. It was that when he told me what Pat had asked, I remembered that Pat had come to me after watching a story about the Terri Schiavo case on TV and made the same request of me.

Schiavo was a Florida woman who'd lapsed into a vegetative state after suffering a massive heart attack at the age of twenty-seven. Eight years later, after all treatments to revive her had failed, her husband petitioned the court to remove her feeding tube. Her parents, however, believed she was still conscious, and fought his petition. A prolonged court battle ensued. Seven years later — fifteen years after her heart attack — the court ordered that her feeding tube be permanently removed. She died thirteen days later.

When Pat came to me after seeing that Schiavo story, I was totally dismissive of him. I told him I didn't understand why he would even let his mind go to such a dark place, and scolded him for indulging in negative thinking. But when Pat's friend told me about Pat's request, I knew instantly why Pat didn't argue with me that night. He knew it would be pointless to argue. He knew I'd never give up on him without a fight. He must have gone to his friend to make sure that his wishes would be honoured.

His friend and I spoke for a long while that evening.

When it was time for him to leave, I thanked him for coming, told him I took his words very seriously, and said I knew he'd come by out of his love for Pat. I told him how sorry I was that he'd had to live with the burden of the knowledge he'd carried for so long, and assured him I had no intention of letting Pat languish in a vegetative state indefinitely. I also told him that although it was hard for me to hear what he had to say, it was also a great relief, because even though I wasn't yet ready to let Pat go, when the time came, I knew I had his permission.

His friend's visit forced me to confront several deeply troubling questions. I struggled to understand how I could have forgotten that conversation with Pat. It seemed inconceivable to me that I didn't recall it when I was contemplating what to do about his living will. I also wrestled with why I'd been so quick to dismiss his concerns after he saw the Schiavo story that night. In light of what his friend had told me, I was ashamed I'd brushed Pat off so cavalierly. He obviously had strong feelings on the subject. But the most disturbing thought of all was that I now knew beyond a shadow of a doubt that my husband did not want to be kept alive and I couldn't bring myself to let him go. Why? What was holding me back?

In the following months, I wrestled mightily with that question. I had no doubt that when I'd told Pat not to let his mind go to such a dark place, I believed I was acting in his best interests. But after his friend's visit, I began to wonder if my motivations had been more complicated than I'd realized. What if the real reason I'd shuttered that conversation so quickly wasn't because I thought it was counter-productive for Pat to indulge in such negative thoughts, but because *I* found them unbearable to contemplate? What if I'd shooed him away because the prospect of losing him to such a random act of fate was too terrifying for me to entertain? What if I'd buried that memory in some subterranean level of my consciousness because the idea was unspeakable for me? And what if that memory had failed to surface at the decisive moment because the dissonance between his wishes and my needs was too much for me to bear?

I'd always believed that my decision to keep Pat alive had been driven by my unwavering love for him and my unerring faith that he'd defy the odds. But after his friend came to see me I began to understand that as much as I loved Pat, as devoted as I'd been to helping him recover, my decision to keep him alive was not a selfless act. It was deeply bound up with my own needs.

Pat and I had been together since we were fourteen. The prospect of living in a world in which he longer existed was unimaginable to me. For even though he was lost to me in any meaningful sense, even though I knew he was never coming back, even though as long as he lingered between life and death, my own life would remain a desert, as long as he was breathing he was still alive. *He was there.* If I let him go, he would be gone. And then we'd no longer be together. But my fears went even deeper. Our lives had been intertwined for so long — if I ended Pat's life, it felt to me as if I would also be ending my own. So, for me, having Pat there but not there was better than not having him there at all. Even the ghost of him was better than the alternative.

I THOUGHT A LOT ABOUT DESTINY that year and how it had brought such sadness and pain into my life. But I also thought about the moments of grace it had brought: how Dr. Jane had come into my life just when I needed her the most; how that nurse at Hamilton General had comforted me when I was panicking that Pat was going to die. I'd tried desperately to find that nurse afterwards to thank her for her kindness, but I could never track her down. And then I saw her at Joe Brant on the morning of Pat's transfer back from Chedoke. She vanished into the crowd before I could reach her, but her presence at yet another of my darkest moments lifted my spirits again. I can't explain why I found her presence so uplifting. All I know is that at both of those moments I felt as if an angel had descended from the heavens to give me strength precisely when I needed it the most.

Some people would say those encounters were just random coincidences, and maybe that's all they were. Still, they made me feel less alone. Somehow they helped me see the universe not just as a randomly cruel place, but as a benevolent one as well, and that insight was pivotal for me.

For a long time the only explanation I could find for why Pat had lost his life was so that I would have to spend the rest of mine feeling lost and broken-hearted. If I were to find the strength to let Pat go and move forward with my life, I didn't just have to let go of the past — I had to be able to envision the future. But when I tried to visualize my life after Pat, all I saw was darkness. Gradually, however, I began to see that letting go of Pat's life didn't have to mean the end of mine.

For two years I'd tried desperately to prop open the door to the past. If I succeeded in keeping that door ajar, when Pat recovered he could walk through it. And then we could walk forward together into the future. But in spite of all my efforts, I couldn't prevent that door from closing. It was as if an immutable force had summoned all of its powers to slam it shut. For the first time, it occurred to me that maybe the reason I couldn't keep that door open was because it was meant to close. And until it did, another couldn't open.

For the first time, a crack of light shone through the darkness. Because if it was true that some things were just meant to be, then maybe it was my destiny to meet Pat and share the years I'd shared with him and have the kids we'd had together. And now maybe I was meant to enter a different phase of life. To travel another path than the one I thought I was on. And if that was the case, then why couldn't it be one of hope and promise?

IN THE END, there was no bolt of lightning. No thundering voice came down from the heavens to tell me it was time. I just knew. In February I'd moved Pat into a long-term facility at the end of our street, and after that, his health began to deteriorate. It was one thing after another.

Near the end, when Pat was very sick, my mom, a girlfriend and I went to Toronto for the evening to have dinner and see a show. I knew I had to make a decision soon. I knew I was just prolonging the inevitable. And yet, in spite of everything I knew, I couldn't bring myself to take Pat off life-support.

As we were exiting the parking lot, I noticed an object glittering at my feet. I bent down and discovered it was a necklace. There was a diamond cross dangling from the chain.

I can't explain why finding that necklace felt meaningful to me, any more than I can explain why that chance encounter with the nurse who'd comforted me at Hamilton General lifted my spirits a second time. All I know is that before I could let Pat go I needed some external reassurance that fate was guiding my hand. For whatever reason, that lost necklace that I found gave me the reassurance I needed.

I asked the doctors to take Pat off life-support in mid-August. They removed his feeding tube, deactivated his ICD and put him on a morphine patch. I took the kids to see him one last time before he died. They didn't know it would be the last time they'd see their dad. They were too young to understand what was really happening. "Oh Mom, do we have to?" they chorused. "It's so boring."

It was a Friday night in late August. There was a fair on the grounds of Tansley Woods that night. I said, "Come say hi to your dad and give him a kiss. Then I'll take you to the fair."

I stood at his bedside, struggling to maintain my

composure and watched as one by one, my children kissed their dad goodbye. "Okay," I said. "Who wants to go on the Ferris wheel and get some cotton candy?"

HE DIED THE NEXT DAY, August 22, four days before Hailey's twelfth birthday. When death was near, I asked our minister to perform last rites. Then I crawled into bed beside him and held him close until he took his last breath.

CHAPTER TWELVE

Nowhere to Hide

THE DAY AFTER PAT'S FUNERAL, I flew to the Bahamas with my mom and the kids. I couldn't just go back to work the next day. I had to draw a line, make a break, put some distance between the past and whatever lay ahead of me. The following morning, as I sat on my hotel balcony staring out at the ocean, I felt many feelings, but mainly I felt a profound sense of relief. Pat was finally at peace. And I had been at his side until his last breath.

As I sat there reflecting on the crossroads to which my life had come, it occurred to me that I was now officially a widow. I didn't like that word. Just thinking about it made me uncomfortable. It conjured up an image of an old woman dressed in black. A woman whose life was over.

I was too young to be a widow.

I glanced down at my wedding band and engagement ring. What was I supposed to do with those? Should I keep wearing them? Take them off? Wear them for a while? What were the rules?

I had no idea how to be a widow. I knew how to be a wife, a mother, a vice-president. I didn't have any trouble fulfilling those roles. But widow? Where did I start?

I sat there mulling these questions for a long time. After a while, a thought nudged its way into my consciousness. Maybe I hadn't sought this title. Maybe no one had asked me if I wanted this job. But one thing I did know how to do was face the unknown. I could handle it. *Lisa*, I told myself. *You can do this. You just have to make a fresh start.*

After the previous two years, I was desperate to move forward, driven to make some kind of change in my life. I called my real estate agent as soon as I returned home and told her I wanted to look at cottages. Buying a cottage felt like the kind of change I was looking for. Pat and I had talked about buying a cottage one day. If we couldn't realize that dream together, I'd realize it on my own.

In September, my mom and I drove up to Muskoka to look at properties. We looked at a few that day, but I didn't see any I liked. On the drive home we were chatting when she asked me whether I'd seen the new house that had just gone up for sale near hers.

I was surprised to hear that news. My mom and I

often went for walks along the lake near where she lived. I thought I knew every house for sale on that route.

"What house? Where?"

"Near us."

"Why don't I know about it?"

"The sign just went up."

"Are you sure?"

She assured me that it had.

"Let's go and see it when we get home."

I called my agent from the car and asked her to meet us there.

I had no intention of looking at houses that day. I certainly didn't have any intention of buying one. I had cottages on my mind. But I was craving a change, and the moment I pulled into the driveway I knew that house was the change I'd been looking for. After we took the tour I told my agent to put in an offer.

When she called the next day I was sure she was calling to say that the deal had gone through. Instead, she said the owners had decided to pull the house off the market. They feared they'd underpriced it.

It wasn't until I felt the crushing blow of that disappointment that I realized how desperately I wanted to move. It wasn't until then that I truly understood how urgently I needed to get out of the Millcroft house and leave the past behind. I had to escape that house. It was freighted with memories of Pat. I couldn't bear to live in it one more minute without him.

I tried to tell myself another house would come along. I tried to convince myself it would be an even better house.

But I didn't have the energy. Now that I knew how desperately I wanted to move, I had no patience for waiting.

This time, though, the gods were smiling upon me. A couple of days later I was in the middle of a strategy session at work when my agent called to say the owners had changed their minds. They'd accepted my offer. The house was mine.

I'D STARTED PREPARING THE KIDS for Pat's death after Dr. Jane sent him back to Joe Brant. I'd told them that if Daddy didn't get better he'd go to heaven. They were familiar with the concept of heaven. Pat and I had told them heaven was the place you went after you died. It was where his mom and my dad were. The kids' biggest concern for Pat had always been whether he'd walk again, so I told them that if he went to heaven when he arrived he'd look the same way they remembered him looking before he had his heart attack.

The morning after he died, I gathered them together with my family at my side to give them the news. "Remember I told you that if Daddy didn't get well he would go to heaven?" I said. "Well, last night he went to heaven. And remember I told you that when he was in heaven he'd be able to see his mommy again? Well he's probably having a dance with her right now." When I finished speaking the kids just sat there staring at me. Nobody said a word. Hailey was the first to break the silence. "Mom," she said, "that's so nice. Can we go swimming now?"

I DIDN'T CRY AT PAT'S FUNERAL. Somehow I managed to hold it together. I didn't want his funeral to be a sad affair. I wanted it to be a celebration of life. So that's what I called it. The church was so packed we had to put people on the grass out front and hook up speakers outside. The girls stood up and said a few words about their dad. Hailey talked about how she and Pat were the funny ones in the family. Chloe talked about how she always stood on his feet when they danced. Mya talked about how he always gave her donuts when I wasn't looking.

In my eulogy, I spoke about Pat as a husband and father and about how much the kids and I would miss him, but I also talked about how seeing his life slip away in an instant had changed me forever. I said that so often in life we let the smallest, stupidest matters consume us, but that the past two years had taught me what truly mattered. I told them I didn't want Pat to have lost his life in vain. I said I wanted what had happened to him to serve as a reminder to everyone sitting there to value their own lives more. I said I wanted every person in that chapel to leave there that day with a sense of strength and purpose they didn't possess before and make the most of every moment they had on this planet. Then the kids and I walked down the centre aisle of the church with "Ramble On" by Led Zeppelin cranked to full volume.

AS SOON AS I KNEW WE WERE MOVING, I kicked into high gear. I had the house staged. After our house sold, I sold off every stick of furniture we owned. Then I furnished the new house from scratch. We moved in a few weeks before Christmas. Once we were in, I began setting up. Then I crashed.

I thought living in a house without memories of Pat would be therapeutic. Instead, all it did was remind me he was gone. When the pain hit, it hit hard. That first Christmas in the new house I felt more alone than I have ever felt at any other time in my life. It was a deep, existential aloneness, far worse than any I'd experienced in the previous two years. It wasn't until after we'd moved that I realized what was happening.

I thought I'd already grieved for Pat. I thought the worst was over. It was only when I felt the pain of that aloneness that I realized until then I'd been grieving other losses: the loss of hope, the loss of my illusions, the loss of the life I'd known. I'd missed Pat desperately during those two years. But as much as I'd longed for him to awaken, when he was alive I still had a husband. Now my husband was gone. For the last four months I'd been frantically trying to distract myself from the finality of his loss. Now that loss was staring me in the face. In one way or another I'd been running from that moment since the night he'd collapsed. Now there was nowhere to hide.

I'd repressed my feelings for so long that when they finally surfaced they were so intense and chaotic I had no idea what to do with them. Going to work, caring for Pat, raising the kids: that I could handle. But this? This was beyond me. I had to find some way to contain my emotions. What was I in for? How long would these feelings last? Was the pain going to get worse? All I could think to do was google the grieving process.

The first thing I learned was that there wasn't any playbook for how to grieve. People grieved in different ways. But there were commonalities. I had five stages ahead of me, and people could grieve for years but the first year was generally the hardest. The pain was rawest then.

I told myself okay, I'm in for another year of this. I've spent the last four months in denial. I can cross that one off my list. For the next few months I'll be angry. Then I'll start praying to make the pain go away. Then I'll be depressed. I tried very hard to organize my grief. I wanted to parcel it off into neat, manageable segments. But grief, I discovered, can't be organized.

Once my feelings forced their way to the surface, they were in no mood to show mercy. I cried more that year than I'd cried in the previous two. My emotions were all over the place. Every time I had to fill out a form that year and tick off the widow box I felt sick to my stomach. Even today, I can't stand ticking that box. It's not that I haven't come to terms with Pat's loss. It's just that I've never adjusted to the word "widow." I don't think I ever will.

The first Christmas Eve in the new house, I was furious with Pat for abandoning me. I hurled invective at him in my head all the time: How could you do this to me? How could you make me a widow and leave me to raise four kids alone? I stuffed pillows under the covers to make the bed feel less empty. Some days I'd awaken and forget he was gone until I looked over and saw the lump in the bed. I didn't feel the need to stuff pillows in the bed when he was still alive. I could tell myself his absence was only temporary then. Now that space felt like a yawning void.

After Christmas it was our anniversary. It would have been our sixteenth, and now that he was gone I had to stop counting. Only I wasn't ready to stop counting. If I stopped counting, I had to accept I was a widow and I wasn't ready to accept my new reality. Not yet. I decided I wanted an anniversary band. I told myself I deserved an anniversary band. Pat would have bought me one for our fifteenth anniversary if he'd been able. All my friends had anniversary bands. Why shouldn't I have one, too? I bought myself the band. I wore it for six months. Then one day I looked down at my hand and it just made me feel sad so I took it off.

I thought buying that ring meant I was carrying on with our traditions. It took me a while to understand that what I was really trying to do was rewind time. I wanted to be the person I was when Pat was still alive. It was still too soon for me to understand I'd never be that person again, and that I wouldn't actually want to be her. I wore my wedding band for a year and a half after he died, though. It was my shield. It kept people from asking questions I wasn't yet ready to answer.

I booked myself up more than ever that year. I'd always found it hard to be around couples, but that first year after Pat died I found it excruciating. I couldn't bear to sit with an empty chair beside me.

After Pat was gone I expected people to gather around me. When someone dies, that's what people do. They drop by. They bring food. They help you through. But people didn't gather round. They fell away. And that really upset me. My husband had passed away. How could people behave as if nothing had changed? It took me time to understand that they'd made the same assumptions I had. After Pat died, they thought I was done with my grieving. That I was finally free to get on with my life. They didn't understand you couldn't grieve for someone who still had a beating heart.

After Pat died, some of my friends said nothing. I guess they had no idea what to say or were worried about saying the wrong thing, but their silence hurt me the most. And yet, one year my girlfriends organized a girls' night on Valentine's Day so I wouldn't have to be alone that night, and another time my maid of honour invited me to dinner on what would have been my anniversary, so instead of feeling sad that night, I enjoyed a lovely evening out with a friend. Sometimes people sent me a note out of the blue to say they were thinking of me. I can't tell you how much those gestures meant. Ever since I was fourteen, I'd had someone in my life who cared about where I was and what I was doing on any given moment of every single day. Just knowing that I was in another person's thoughts buoyed my spirits immeasurably.

BY AUGUST 2010, almost a year had passed since Pat's death. By all appearances the kids were doing fine. To set my mind at ease I'd had them assessed by a child psychologist after we'd returned from the Bahamas and she'd told me they were coping well. I think they'd grown so used to not having Pat around they didn't experience his death as traumatic.

That summer, I rented a cottage, got my boating licence and the kids and I spent a couple of weeks in Muskoka. It was the first time we'd gone to the cottage without Pat. Another first.

I'd just walked into my office on the Monday morning after our vacation when my assistant told me our COO was on the phone from Memphis. The COO was one of my mentors. He was the one who'd counselled me to treat every interaction with anyone above my pay grade as a mini-interview for a promotion. I was curious why he was calling. I told my assistant I'd take the call in my office, and said hello.

"Hi, Lisa. Congratulations."

"Congratulations? For what?"

"You're the new president of FedEx Express Canada."

"*President?* What do you mean? Don't you want to interview me?"

"Lisa," he laughed, "you've been interviewing for eighteen years."

IN 2011, WHEN I WAS APPROACHED to participate in *Undercover Boss Canada*, I had to decide between playing it safe or going for broke. I definitely had my reservations about participating in a reality TV show. The show was completely unscripted and I wouldn't be privy to the shooting schedule until the last possible moment, so I'd have no idea where I'd be going each day, whom I'd be meeting or the role I'd be playing. Talk about working without a net!

I'm not a huge TV watcher, but I wanted to make sure that the show was the real deal, so I researched who the producers were and learned how the show was put together. I was especially concerned about how my employees would react to me going undercover, so I reached out to some of the CEOs who'd done previous episodes of the show and asked them to tell me about their experiences. Did they have any regrets or advice? Would they have done anything differently? How did their employees react to the undercover part? Did they feel as if they'd been tricked?

Not one CEO warned me off participating. In fact, everyone single person I approached told me that doing the show had been one of the best experiences of their lives. They told me that they had worried about their employees' reactions, too, but their concerns had turned out to be a complete non-issue. I decided that the show was the real deal, and I signed on.

As far as my employees on the show knew, they were participating in a new reality show that was to be a competition. They believed that the producers were going to take someone who wasn't currently in the workforce and throw that person into different work environments. One day they'd work at FedEx Express Canada, another at Tim Hortons, another at McDonald's.

The employees' understanding was that their job was to train the novice for a day. They were to teach that person everything they possibly could in one day about how to do their job. At the end, all the employees who trained the person in the various companies would be flown to head office. The trainee would choose the company where she wanted to work based on the one who'd done the best job of training her. If she chose to work at FedEx Express Canada, our company would win the competition.

Of course, not a word of that was true.

The producers arranged for me to be disguised as a mother of two who'd recently returned to the workforce. Then the costume and makeup people went to work on me. Between my mousy-brown hair extensions, frumpy glasses and puffy work wear I was so well disguised, none of my employees had a clue that they were training the president of the company.

I had to do all the jobs that they did: sort packages, load trucks, make deliveries. In many cases, I had to master tasks that often take weeks or months to perfect, like using a PowerPad. (Our couriers are skilled at using them. I wasn't quite as adept.)

In one of the segments I had to do a night shift with our sort team and sort and track containers full of packages as they were coming off the aircraft. The challenge was to make sure that every container was accounted for and that none got left behind on the plane. The work was so physically and mentally demanding I couldn't keep up! I was completely out of my league.

Not surprisingly, I messed up. Nobody was going to nominate me for employee of the month. But my coworkers were patient with me and when the show aired, my mistakes didn't seem to matter to viewers. What mattered was that I was willing to put myself out there. I was game.

Obviously, when people know that you're the president of the company, they're more guarded about what they're willing to say in your presence. Travelling undercover allowed me to see a side of my employees that I would otherwise never have seen. Taking that risk and throwing myself heart and soul into that experience gave me real insight into what was and wasn't working at the grassroots level in our company, not to mention a new admiration for what our employees do every day.

Had I not worked inside the Kelowna, B.C., station on the show, I wouldn't have known how desperately it needed expansion. No doubt I would have learned about the situation eventually, but it would have taken a lot longer for that information to filter up to my level. Seeing the problem firsthand allowed me to take action faster. And had I not witnessed how long it was taking my employees to process waybills manually, I wouldn't have understood the urgency of automating. I also gained insight into the struggles that we all face as human beings every day and made friendships that I believe will last for the rest of my life.

PARTICIPATING IN *UNDERCOVER BOSS CANADA* turned out to be one the most meaningful experiences of my life. When I signed on to do the show, my primary goal (besides not embarrassing myself!) was to represent my company well. But when I signed on, I had no idea how much participating would teach me that I wasn't alone. That part has been a bonus.

When you suffer a loss like the one I endured, for a long time you feel as if you're the only person on earth who has suffered such pain. You know it's absurd to think that way, but loss can be profoundly isolating, and for a long time that is how I felt.

When I took part in the show, I met employees who were dealing with their own loss and pain. Hearing about their struggles and seeing how bravely they were carrying on helped me put my own loss into perspective. Their stories reminded me that I wasn't alone, and bequeathed me a deep feeling of connectedness to all other human beings on the planet. I also realized, even more than I had before, that sadness and loss are a part of the human condition. Like happiness and joy, both will touch everyone's lives at some point. That is a given, no matter how wonderful other people's lives seem on Facebook or Instagram.

As time moves forward, I think less about the sadness and loss in my life and more about the happiness and joy I was so lucky to have with Patrick for all the years I did. When I think about him, I don't picture him lying in a hospital bed. I picture the nights he'd come home from work when he was in town and come up behind me at the stove while I was getting dinner ready and pull back my hair and give me a kiss me on the back of my neck. It still gives me goosebumps remembering that.

I think, too, about all the people I met on my journey — people I'd never have met had it not been for the loss

I suffered, but who, in the knowing, have inestimably enriched my life. People like Dr. Jane, to whom I turned for guidance and solace in Pat's final days. Her hand was on my shoulder until the end. Others, too, many others, from the nurses and caregivers who cared so lovingly for Pat to the friends and colleagues who cared so lovingly for me. So many people stood by my side through my darkest hour. I will never forget them.

CHAPTER THIRTEEN

Finding My Happiness

IT'S BEEN TEN YEARS since the night my life changed forever. Losing Pat has been the most painful experience of my life. But it has also been the most transformative. I believe my ordeal has made me a better person and parent, and not a day goes by when I don't bring the lessons I've learned as a widow and single mother to my job as a leader. The wisdom I've gained travelling this path has forever altered my way of being in the world.

I have learned so many lessons. The most indelible is this: destiny doesn't give you any warning when it comes calling. It just shows up one day and comes crashing into your life. You have to cope with the mayhem the best way you can. But destiny also comes bearing gifts, and one it gave me was the knowledge that I possessed deep reservoirs of strength within me — reservoirs I had no idea existed. It showed me where to find them, how to tap into them and how to replenish and forge new ones when they were tapped out. I was far more prepared than I knew or had any reason to expect when destiny came calling. As it turned out, I'd been preparing for destiny's arrival all my life.

I used to think life adhered to a set of rules, and if I followed them, life would go largely according to plan. But the randomness of Pat's fate and my powerlessness to change it shattered every assumption I had about the way the world worked. The aftershocks shook me to the core of my identity. When the dust settled, a different person crawled out of the rubble. Although I would never have wished to endure the suffering fate thrust upon me, today I view where it has taken me with gratitude and wonder.

I have learned what it means to have humility. I used to think I understood what humility meant. I thought it meant not letting my title go to my head. But in truth, I had no idea what humility meant — at least not in any deep sense. Before Pat fell ill, I thought we were immune to life's darker forces. When life threw a brick through our window in the form of Pat's illness, it wasn't just that I couldn't fathom how something so terrible had happened to him. I couldn't fathom how it had happened to us. So I refused to believe that it had. I thought there weren't any limits to what I could accomplish. When it turned out there were indeed limits to what I could control, I was forced to acknowledge I wasn't the person I thought I was. It was the most humbling experience of my life.

In retrospect, it was absurd to think I could stop fate in its tracks. And yet, that is what I believed. I thought all I had to do to bring Pat back was apply the skills that had taken me so far in the business world. I didn't want to believe destiny was beyond my command.

I thought all I had to do to achieve my goal was remain positive. If I stayed strong, if I never wavered, Pat would get a miracle. When my optimism failed to bring about his recovery, I had to accept that optimism had its limits. I'm still an optimist. I will always be an optimist. Embracing positive thinking, even in the darkest of times, is central to my worldview. But I no longer believe that a sunny attitude can solve everything. Now I understand that some things are just meant to be, and I have come to terms with that reality.

But while those skills might not have helped me bring back Pat, I couldn't have made it through my journey without them and the coping skills I developed. These skills gave me control over my life when I had no reason to believe I had any. They allowed me to put one foot in front of the other when all I longed to do was curl up in a ball. They saw me through Hailey's birthday party and that awful May weekend. They helped me get Pat into rehab and convince the Joe Brant staff to let me bring him home. Many times over my life skills saved me.

I hung on too long. I know I did. I had to learn to let go and accept that it was time. Knowing when to let go is fundamental to so many of the choices you have to make in life, whether you're leaving behind a job, a relationship or a loved one. Acknowledging when it's time to walk away is never easy, but you have to face that moment when it comes.

Letting go of Pat was the hardest decision I've ever had to make. Arriving at that place took time and strength and painful self-examination. But the process taught me so much about myself. I discovered that you can have ambitions for another person that can be driven by deep love and devotion, and not realize that your ambitions for them aren't necessarily what they want or value. Love isn't about overruling the other person. Love is about respecting their wishes.

And yet, I don't regret the choices I made. Any other choice would have been unthinkable for me. I had to believe Pat would recover. I had to do everything within my power to see that he did. If I hadn't made the choices I did, I'd never have been able to live with myself. Nor would I have found a way to embrace life again.

I have learned to have empathy. I didn't lack empathy before Pat had his heart attack. I have always been a sensitive person. Now I just have a much deeper capacity for empathy. I'm less inclined to judge others than I once was and more willing to forgive them. I have more compassion for myself, too. I still push myself. I will always try to go above and beyond in whatever I do. But if I falter or fail, I'm more willing to forgive myself.

I used to think that asking for help was a sign of weakness, but now I'm much more comfortable asking for it, and much more comfortable receiving it. I could not possibly have survived the ordeal I've been through without others' support. I still value my independence, but I now know that radical sovereignty is not the answer. If you are open to receiving help, it is all around you, and you will be that much stronger for having accepted it. No matter how independent you are — or prize yourself on being — no one gets through life on their own, nor should they aspire to.

I have learned to live in the moment. People often say they will value every moment after they suffer a life-threatening illness or loss. I know I vowed to do that after my dad died. But in fact, after he died I was so terrified of wasting a moment of my life that what drove me was fear. I didn't live in the moment afterwards. I was too busy living in the future. I spent the next fifteen years pushing myself to get somewhere other than where I was — whether it was to land the next promotion, have the next kid or move into the next house.

I still believe it's important to have plans and goals in life. But it took seeing Pat's life vanish before my eyes to truly understand what it means to live in the moment. I don't look back now because the past is gone and I don't live there anymore. I don't worry about the future because I've learned worrying about the future is a waste of energy. All it does is rob you of the chance to experience the beautiful present.

I have learned to live with ambiguity. That lesson has been an especially tough one for me to learn. I'm a goal-oriented person by nature. Dealing with shades of grey does not come easily to me. But Dr. Jane taught me that to be alive means to live with uncertainty. She helped me see that the best way to deal with life's darkness was not to pretend that it didn't exist but to try and find some way to live around it with hope. She never gave me false hope. But she never took my hope away either. She never told me that what I was seeing was all I could ever expect to see. She understood. She held my hand. She walked with me.

I have learned it's impossible to deny the pain of grief. You can outrun it for a while. You can put people between you and your loneliness. You can even become the president of a company to keep it at bay. But grief can't be avoided. Eventually it will demand your full attention. The only way to get through it is day by day, month by month, year by year, by focusing on what you have to be thankful for — and not on what has been taken from you. And then one day you look up and realize that the worst is behind you.

Most of all, I've learned that I am resilient. Just as great leaders can inspire you to take on challenges you'd never consider taking on, adversity can bring out the best in you. Discovering that I could cope with unimaginable suffering, and bounce back from my loss even stronger than I was before, is the greatest gift adversity has given me.

I'M HAPPY TO REPORT the kids are thriving. I like to think that Pat would be proud of the people they're becoming. At the moment we have four dogs, a rabbit and a fish named Shinequa, but the pet situation is fluid. The kids don't mention Pat a lot, but there's no predicting when the subject will come up. Once we were away for March Break and they started asking questions, so we talked for a few hours over lunch. They have photographs of him in their rooms, and we visit his grave on his birthday and Father's Day. He lives on in our hearts and memories.

Like any parent who has lost a partner, I try to be both a mother and father to the kids. I especially try to be a father to Jack, who was three at the time of his dad's heart attack and thus has no memories of him. When he has a hockey game, sometimes I'm the only mom in the locker room. I try to listen to what the dads say to their sons after a game and say that to Jack, but of course I can't replace his dad, so I also try to make sure he has strong male influences in his life.

The toughest moments are the ones when I remember what the kids are missing by not having him in their lives. The night before Mya's grade eight graduation, I found her sobbing in the bathroom. She really missed her dad that night because he wouldn't be there to dance the father-daughter dance with her. That was hard. So was the year Jack's hockey team won the championship and I went running out on the ice with all the other moms and dads to take pictures and I saw how proud he was. I so wished Pat could have been there to share that moment. I didn't want Jack to see me crying, so I concentrated on shooting the video. I'm the family videographer now, too.

Hailey and Jack are off the beta blockers now. They doctors ruled out a genetic cause for Pat's heart attack and they took them off the meds. They don't know what caused his heart attack, but whatever it was, it started and ended with him.

I still keep busy and throw parties. When Hailey graduated from high school, she wanted the grad party at our house. First the guest list was at thirty. Then it went to forty. Then it went to eighty. Chloe wanted to hold her Sweet Sixteen on the same weekend. I could have put my foot down and said no way, it's too much. But I didn't say no. I said yes. We had the grad party on the Friday and the Sweet Sixteen on the Saturday. I didn't agree to have both parties because I'm a pushover. I agreed because my kids missed out on having a dad. I want them to feel they have a kickass mom.

Once the kids got older and Hailey learned to drive, there wasn't enough work for Jojo to do during the day, so we said goodbye to our beloved nanny. When people hear I don't have a nanny they wonder how I manage. I manage in part by relying on my parents for backup. Without their help, I couldn't do it. I also manage by delegating — just as I do at work. The kids have to clean up their rooms, put their laundry away, walk the dogs, unpack the groceries, unload the dishwasher, take out the garbage and bring the empty garbage bins back from the end of the driveway so I don't find them halfway down the street on a windy day. They hate doing their chores, but they know if I come home and there's stuff on the counter or the dogs haven't been walked, I will lose my mind. Then they'll have to sit through a family meeting on Sunday evening at seven o'clock. They hate having to sit through family meetings.

The family meeting has proven to be a very useful motivational tool indeed.

Once Hailey began to drive, I told her, here's the deal: if I'm paying for your gas so you can drive around with your friends, you have to help out with the chores. She was home from school one week when Jack needed new skates. I asked her to take him. She texted me from the sporting goods store with three options, took that responsibility off my list, and Jack had his new skates for his big game that Sunday. When she's home from university, she'll text me from the road to see if I need her to pick something up. That's how we roll.

Like most single parents, I have to play good cop and bad cop. Sometimes I have to be the heavy whether I like it or not. If I see the kids have been negligent when I walk in the front door, I'm on them right away. I run a really tight ship. But we have lots of parties on that ship.

The kids are ready for me to meet someone. They've given me permission. To be honest, they're pushing me: "If you want to go on a date and bring home a new dad, Mom, it's okay with us. We want to come to your wedding."

I'm ready for a new relationship, but meeting someone is not my top priority. Maybe it will happen and maybe it won't. If it doesn't, I won't be disappointed. My happiness doesn't depend on it. I'm open but not looking. Ready but not waiting. There's a difference.

Sometimes, though, it feels as if everyone else is waiting on my behalf. It's not even funny how interested others are in my love life. I'm asked if I'm seeing someone all the time. When someone asked me that question recently and I said that I wasn't, she adopted this pitying tone and said, "Don't worry. You'll meet someone and then you'll be happy." I guess it's hard for some people to understand that we all have different notions of happiness and that our ideas can change over time.

I used to fear my nights alone. Now I crave them. Between my business dinners, speaking engagements and travel schedule, I rarely have a night off. If I do manage to steal one for myself, I'd rather spend it at home with my kids, reading a good book or catching up with a girlfriend. I'd have to meet a pretty special guy to entice me to give up one of those opportunities.

One thing I do know: If I have a free night, I'm not going to spend it on a blind date. I have nothing against blind dates. I'm just too much of a romantic to meet someone in such an unromantic way! I'll have to bump into him at the gas station or in an airport lounge. Destiny has to play a role. I feel the same way about online dating. Again, I make no judgments. I know lots of people who have met their partners online. My brother met the love of his life on a dating site. It's just not for me.

There's a real freedom in being content with the person you are and the life you're living. And I do feel free. I feel free because I've learned that aloneness isn't a physical state. It's a state of mind. I don't share my life with another adult. In that sense, I'm alone. But you don't need to share your life with another adult for your life to be rich and rewarding.

If I do meet someone who interests me and I choose to be with that person, I won't compare him to Pat. I carry Pat in my heart always, but the love we shared was between us, and that love is in the past. If another love comes along, it will be in the present, and I would never burden a new love with the weight of one that has passed. No one should have to carry that burden. Besides, what I'm talking about has less to do with comparing than with refusing to settle. At a certain time in my life I had something special. Now I'm looking for other things.

I still miss Pat of course. I will always miss him. But time has leavened the pain of his loss. When my pain was still fresh, people told me that time would heal all my wounds. Then, their words felt like an affront. Now I know those words are true. Of all the lessons I've learned, that one may be the most surprising. And yet, no matter how well-intentioned those words may be, I still think they're the worst words you can say to someone who's traumatized. That person has to come to that understanding in their own time and their own way.

People sometimes ask me how you get over losing the love of your life. I tell them I don't think you ever do: grief doesn't have a finish line. I think you just learn how to live around the loss. And be grateful for the time you had together. I'm deeply grateful for the time I had with Pat. Even if I'd known what destiny had in store, I would not trade the years we had for anything. Not just because of the bond we forged and the kids we raised. Because I never lost the feeling I had for him from the moment I first laid eyes on him in geography class.

Through all our years together, our romance never faded. I had that feeling all through high school. I had it in university when he showed up at my dorm. I had it when he pulled up at the cottage and walked in the door after being on the road. Pat was right in what he said on the last night we spoke. We *were* blessed. We had more joy together than most people find in a lifetime.

Today, I live my life with a grateful heart. I still feel blessed. All that's changed is my idea of what that word means. Today, I consider myself blessed if my kids and I are healthy and safe. That's all I need to feel that the gods are smiling upon me. I didn't get the happy ending I pictured, but I got a happy ending nonetheless. I have learned that happiness is not something you can get from a person, place or thing. Happiness is a state of mind — one that you must cultivate every single day.

Acknowledgements

AS WITH EVERY GOAL I've set out to accomplish in my life, the path I travelled to write this book began with a baby step. After Pat died, many people encouraged me to write a book, but I didn't know if my story would interest a wider audience. One Sunday morning I was sitting in my home office pondering the idea, when I decided to take my first step towards finding out. I contacted my speechwriter, Scott Feschuk, to see if I could enlist his help. Scott said that as much as he'd love to work with me on the project, he knew someone he thought would be perfect. Her name was Wendy Dennis. It was, to say the least, a fortuitous connection. Had our paths not crossed, this book would not exist.

Wendy is an extraordinarily gifted writer, but "ghost-writer" doesn't begin to do justice to the role she played in helping me bring my story to life. Nor does it do justice to the intimacy of our collaboration or the pleasure I took in working so closely with someone with her empathy and creative intelligence. She cared about my story from our first meeting, and she continued to care about it until the book went to press. Her contribution went far beyond her storytelling talents. She guided me through every step of the process, acted as my listener and sounding board, critic and challenger, and drew thoughts and feelings out of me that I didn't even know I had. I'll be forever grateful to Scott for introducing us and to Wendy for joining me on this journey.

I'd also like to thank my agent Carolyn Forde at Westwood Creative Artists, who believed in this project from the get-go, my publisher Jack David of ECW Press, who was also keenly enthusiastic right out of the gate, and the devoted ECW team: Jen Hale, for her brilliant editorial eye, David Caron, Jessica Albert, Rachel Ironstone, Sarah Dunn, Chelsea Humphries, Emma Cole, Troy Cunningham and Tania Craan, who toiled cheerfully and unstintingly behind the scenes to shepherd the book to publication.

I will also be forever indebted to FedEx, not just for hiring an eager but untested university grad and providing me with countless other wonderful opportunities, but for allowing me to run one of their global regions. I don't think too many companies would offer a forty-one-year-old recent widow with four young kids the top job, and I'll be forever grateful to FedEx for their willingness to take that chance on me.

If it takes a village to publish a book, it certainly takes one to run my life, and in that respect I have been exceptionally blessed. I couldn't possibly have arrived at this moment without the love and support of many people.

First, I owe a debt of gratitude to my family and friends, who sustained me through my darkest hours and beyond. I can't name you all, but you know who you are.

I also want to express my heartfelt thanks to my parents and stepparents for their steadfast love, guidance and support. You have all watched over me in different ways, but every one of you has helped me become the person that I am today.

Mom and Ron — you, especially, have served as my anchor. When my world fell apart, you were there to catch me and care for my kids whenever I called. It was your shoulders I leaned on when I lacked the strength to face another day and it was your wisdom I turned to when I was struggling to find my way. I simply could not have made it through without you.

Finally, to my kids, Hailey, Chloe, Mya and Jack: I owe you so much. When our lives turned upside down, you're the reason I got out of bed every morning and you, above all, are the reason I wrote this book. I'm enormously proud of the people you've become, and I know Dad would be enormously proud of you, too. None of us expected the turn our lives would take, but these past ten years we've walked this road together. I've kept my eye on you, you've kept your eye on me, and together we've found resilience.

At ECW Press, we want you to enjoy this book in whatever format you like, whenever you like. Leave your print book at home and take the eBook to go! Purchase the print edition and receive the eBook free. Just send an email to ebook@ecwpress.com and include:

- the book title
- the name of the store where you purchased it
- your receipt number
- your preference of file type: PDF or ePub?

Get the
eBook free!*
*proof of purchase
required

A real person will respond to your email with your eBook attached. And thanks for supporting an independently owned Canadian publisher with your purchase!